I have the privilege of knowing Julie Hunt personally. You won't meet a more transparent person. Her faith life is utterly real. Messy and bare-boned. Full of raw edges and blinding beauty. Julie has walked a road that no one chooses to walk willingly. She lost almost everything the day she lost her soulmate. This book is not just a recounting of her harrowing ordeal. It does not offer easy answers or simple scriptural salve. She asks us to walk along the road with her. Holding hands. Stopping along the path to consider our own frailty and misconceptions about the God who allows us to wander in the thick, dark woods, but the One who also promises a night sky full of stars to help us find our way out. Julie writes with courage because she lives with courage. This book brings hope and promise to any person convinced they cannot get through the long, dark night.

—NICHOLE NORDEMAN, CHRISTIAN RECORDING ARTIST

God gives us all a journey. Some have a clear, straight path while most of us have twists and turns on the road to eternity. This very special book is one woman's journey of perseverance into and out of a turn of events she never asked for or wanted. As with Jesus on the cross, sometimes God allows things He hates to accomplish an outcome He loves. *I'm About to Get Up!* is a guidepost that will help all of us look toward our loving Father—even when it is hard to see tomorrow. You, the reader, will find peace and be blessed by sharing in this journey.

—DR. REGGIE ANDERSON, AUTHOR, *APPOINTMENTS WITH HEAVEN* AND *THE ONE YEAR BOOK OF HEALING*

I had the privilege of witnessing Julie from afar as she navigated the treacherous sea of tragedy. As a wife and mother, she lets us explore, from a close-up view, the days she felt shipwrecked and the days she symbolically had no oars. But she does not leave us there. As a therapist working daily with grief and loss, I appreciate Julie not just telling us, but *showing* us, how to put the sails up once more in life. Her decision to not be defined by the loss, but shaped by it is for all of us. I could not put this book down until the last page.

—MARGARET PHILLIPS, M.S., LICENSED MARITAL AND FAMILY THERAPIST

What a precious gift Julie has given us! How does one navigate the valley of the shadow of death? It can only be revealed by one whose heart and soul, like Noah's ark, has been utterly flooded by the darkest storms and finally left resting on the heights of God's perfect love. The heavy price Julie paid in learning new dance steps will sow hope into all who follow. My advice is to not hurry through this book. Discover, like Julie, the rich treasures to be found on every step of the journey. This book serves as deep encouragement that the greatest treasure is ending up in Abba's lap.

—JOSEPH WATSON, INTERNATIONAL SPEAKER, YOUTH WITH A MISSION

I'm About to Get Up!

{ PERSEVERING THROUGH LOSS & GRIEF }

JULIE HUNT

Clovercroft Publishing

Published by Clovercroft Publishing, Franklin, Tennessee in association with Larry Carpenter of Christian Book Services, LLC.

Edited by Robert Irvin
Cover and Interior Design by Suzanne Lawing
Author Photo by Alli Worthington

Printed in the United States of America

978-1-942557-75-3

Visit the author's blog at thejuliehunt.com.

Contents

Part One

Part Two

DEDICATION

Father, Son, and Holy Spirit,
I dedicate my whole life to you, and this story would not be
possible without your unfailing, unconditional love.

Gratefully yours, Julie

ACKNOWLEDGMENTS

It's both impractical and impossible to think I could have completed this book without these people in my life.

David (Cooter): two wild and crazy Oklahoma State University journalism brats who God brought together to live life hard, fast, and always in love. You know how much I love you. I'll leave it at that. I cannot wait to see you again!

Aubrey: my beautiful firstborn child! You taught me how to be a mom and how to walk around with my heart inside another person. You are loyal, compassionate, and faith-filled. I'm not sure how I would've gotten through my adult life without you. I love you more deeply than I can describe.

Cameron: my beautiful son! I had no idea that my heart could grow larger until I looked into your face. You make me laugh, cry, scream, and love more deeply. We've shared moments that are beyond words, and I'm so thankful God held our hearts through all the storms. I love you more deeply than I can describe.

Mom, Russ, Jone, and Cindy: I'm grateful for your encouragement. You've always believed in me even when I doubted myself. In my many dark days you brought light to my path and kept me going. Thank you! I love you all.

Dorothy, Mary, and Mark: God's blessing multiplied when I fell in love with David and his wonderful family. You have brought support and encouragement in ways I will never forget. Thank you for opening your hearts and allowing me to jump in and stay!

Charlie and Marlene: You welcomed me with open arms when Kye brought me home to meet his parents. You've been gracious, kind, loving, and supportive, not only with me, but with Aubrey and Cameron too. You've also taught me how to show unconditional love, even when others don't deserve it. I love you both.

Kye: How can I convey how much you mean? This depth of appreciation and love can't be written, only lived. You're my handsome husband, making me laugh again and feel all "junior high school crush" in love! You are God's gift, His special gift of companionship for the second half of life. I'll forever be your Jazz.

Fabulous Friday Friends (FFF): How thankful I am that these thirteen women are beside me through life. Sharing hard times, rejoicing in good times, and loving each other well in between. Thank you for listening and encouraging me to keep writing and finish this book!

Dabney: I wonder how the Father would've gotten my attention had you not nudged me that day with *His* message: "Julie, it's time to write the book! God says it's time." I couldn't ignore such a strong call to action! In obedience, I opened five journals and began to read and type the book God placed inside me. You've been used mightily throughout my life, showing up to speak His work into my life. How I thank you, sweet warrior friend!

A book isn't written or published alone. God sent a team to help me across the finish line.

Larry and the Clovercroft team: Thank you for hope and encouragement that I just might have something in that very first manuscript!

Bob: I understand completely now that when folks thank their editor, they mean so much more than just "thanks." You are an amazing, insightful, and affirming editor. It was easy to trust your help with my project because you're so honorable. You started as my editor, but now I count you as a friend.

Adam: "A word aptly spoken is like apples of gold in settings of silver" (Proverbs 25:11). I needed honest insight, and you gave generously! Thanks to you and Lee Ann!

Lindsey: My marketing guru and book launch expert extraordinaire! You helped me sift through my project and find the message. You're a team builder and focus-finder. I'm so thankful we are walking this path together!

I'm About to Get Up!

"Do not gloat over me, my enemy!
Though I have fallen, I will rise.
Though I sit in darkness,
The Lord will be my light."
MICAH 7:8

If you're wondering, this is not a how-to book on grieving. I can assure you, one doesn't exist. If such a book had been written, I would've found it, devoured it, and actually felt no need to write my own! I get teary-eyed thinking about this today: I remember like it was yesterday, driving to libraries and bookstores, wandering up and down the aisles like some lost little puppy, trying to find a safe place to curl up and recover. I was desperate to find a book, a resource, anyone or *anything* that would help me make sense of the unbearable loneliness, emptiness, and profound sadness I was feeling.

Maybe even someone who had actually faced a doctor who had just climbed off her husband's chest and confirmed the obvious:

"The injuries from the wreck were overwhelming.
Your husband of 22 years is gone.
Life as you've known it is no more."

So is that too much to ask? Is there anyone out there who has survived widowhood and lived to tell about it? Where are the women who've gone through similar circumstances? The young widows, older widows, the widows who still want to live, have fun, and not just wear black and be the odd woman out in a world full of couples? I wanted someone to look me in the eye and tell me—or at least, let me read it in *their* book—"It's going to be OK. You're going to be OK. The madness will eventually stop and you'll have moments of peace, even joy someday." Oh to have been assured by someone I could trust! Someone who'd been there! It would be so comforting to hear or read someone's real, authentic, and honest account of living with tragic loss.

But still, I couldn't find that book.

However, I did find a quote floating around the Internet. I'm not sure whose it is, but it's good, and it goes something like this:

"Write the book you want to read."

That's genius! Exactly what I want to read! But where is this book? I *need* to read this book!

A dear friend gave me a journal about two weeks after my husband's accident. She thought I might find it therapeutic to scrawl my thoughts. She was right. I began journaling my uninvited trip through grief. Jotting down my scribbles and incoherent ramblings. Documenting my maddening thoughts, deepest fears, and all those questions with no answers. As a journalist, I process a lot of my world, including pain, through writing. My sincerest hope, as I recall my experiences and you read them, is to bring into the light what most don't like to talk about, much less read about: the horrific and beautiful glory of loss. I'd like to think God might use my excruciatingly painful road as a helping hand to those who find themselves in a dark hole of grief. It would be an honor bestowed, a beautiful way for me to make some sense of my painful journey.

I came home from that last, disappointing trip to a few more bookstores, sat in my big comfy chair, and asked myself a second time: *What kind of book would I want to read?* And suddenly, my answer was clear. I wanted to read a book about a 43-year-old widow who was lost, heartbroken, inconsolable, and scared. A widow who had an incredibly strong faith in God, but needed understanding, encouragement, time, and love to have a fighting chance to emerge a sane human being. A widow who didn't know how to be needy, wounded, fearful, or afraid, but suddenly felt all of those emotions so deeply that it frightened her. I was a grieving wife, reminding myself to breath every day and hoping I wouldn't forget my socks and shoes when heading to the grocery store. (I once nearly walked out, on my way to the grocery, in yellow bunny slippers!) I muddled through my life in those early months and years of grief solely by the grace of God and countless encouragements from my friends and family.

So, this is that book. It's my story. I journaled through all my heartbreaking moments and my oh my, I'm so glad I did. I'm not sure I could get back to those gut-wrenching battlefields I've crawled through. And frankly, I don't want to ever go back there. It's hard enough just to read what I have written.

But you know what? This not a book about just widowhood, although that was the loss that engaged me in this book-writing mission. It is also about other losses, many personal losses I've experienced. Events like seeing my beloved Papa die right in front of me when I was 11, or my first serious boyfriend dying in a car wreck when he was just 17, and my dad dying suddenly of a stroke when he was only 55. My college roommate and best friend was kidnapped, raped, and murdered. She was 24 and on her way to buy diapers for her 18-month-old son.

And since my husband David's death, two of my closest friends have died of cancer.

Yes, loss has been a prevailing theme of my life, but each

and every one has left increased courage and an undeniable truth: God is always with me and for me, drying every tear and instilling hope for tomorrow.

* * * * * * *

I first read Micah 7:8 in 1997. It resonated with me deeply. I grappled with it for days, poring over it and asking God why this Scripture was jumping off the page for me. Every Bible I've owned in the last nineteen years has this verse underlined, yellow-highlighted, stars in the margins, and "YES!" and "REMEMBER THIS, JULIE!!" also scribbled in those margins.

Close your eyes and imagine with me: here is a seasoned 45-year-old warrior, face down in the mud, on the battlefield, bleeding from lashings of hatred, misunderstanding, and sorrow. Wounds from years of grief, pain, and abuse are carved in her skin. Deep longing through the years stripped away by her enemy. The enemy lets out a mocking laugh as he delivers what he thinks will be the final blow. Laughing, taunting, urging the woman with broken body and spirit: "Just give up."

Then, from deep within my soul, a switch was flipped and strength arose from the pit. Hope connected itself to my will. A battle cry came forth from the depths of my soul and yelled—no screamed—at the enemy: Do not count me out! Do not gloat, make fun of, or laugh at me. You have tried to take me out my entire life, but you have not won. I may be knocked down, worn out, defeated, and in shame, but this is not over.

It may be dark, but God is my light. And . . . I'm About to Get Up!

* * * * * * *

While I'm writing this book for me, I truly hope it helps you or someone you know. (See 2 Corinthians 1:3-5.) May our sorrow not be wasted. We all experience loss of some kind. In Ecclesiastes 7 the Bible says: "death is the destiny of every man, and the *living* should take it to heart" (v. 2, emphasis mine).

So, friend, this is me, giving it a go and "taking it to heart!" One hand holding onto Jesus and the other lifted high, praising my Father, who makes all things well. I'm looking Him straight in the eye while declaring to the world, "This girl made it out alive!" And not just surviving; I'm *living*! I'm a strong, capable, and determined 56-year-old woman who has plundered the enemy and come out of the camp with my inheritance!

I invite you to join me in this journey. While it's not for the faint of heart, it is for the somewhat stubborn, like me, for someone who needs encouragement and evidence that it is possible to live again after the trauma of loss has ravaged your soul. In fact, it's not only possible, it's probable—not because of anything you or I have done, but as evidence that our Father-God is just that good!

Part One

ONE

ALL-AMERICAN FAMILY

The Day the Rain Fell seemed like an ordinary Thursday morning. I'm up at 5 a.m. for my quiet time, and then I fix breakfast for my guys. Our strapping 14-year-old son likes breakfast, but his choices are simple: a bowl of cereal and a piece of toast. Nothing fancy, just like his dad. I think David, his father, had Raisin Bran cereal almost every weekday morning for years.

Ever since his polyp scare we tried to increase our fiber intake. I'd come to learn, in my forties, that it's the little changes that add up to big differences in our lives, especially in our health. Unfortunately, even though he had the goal of increasing fiber in his life, David didn't make it easy! He'd never been a big oatmeal fan.

"It's too gummy and slimy. I don't care for the texture," he'd argue.

"But David, we're supposed to increase your fiber intake! Oatmeal is a great choice for both your colon and heart," I'd counter.

Believe me when I tell you: when David Hunt says he doesn't like something, you don't push it. He *won't* change his mind, not even on a cold wintry morning! His idea of the perfect first meal of the day was what he called a big country breakfast, which was usually our weekend treat. A combination of scrambled eggs, bacon, biscuits, gravy, and sometimes-homemade hash browns—now *that's* what David Hunt called a good breakfast. His momma had trained *and* fed him well. I thought it was cute and really didn't mind a bit. As David always said: "Because I like to eat, I like to cook!" And my goodness, what wife would argue with a husband whose pleasure was to cook for his family on weekends?

On this particular morning, our college student, Aubrey Anne, is fifteen minutes up the road, probably fixing her own breakfast and getting ready for class. She doesn't go by Aubrey Anne, but her daddy liked to call her that. He liked nicknames. He'd given both kids a nickname, as well as one for himself. His was Cooter, and mine was Cooter's Woman. So, so silly! So, back to our morning: my mind is wandering, and I think I should call my daughter later because we haven't talked since Sunday.

In my early morning hours, I read and journal a little and plan the rest of my day. It might look something like this:

- Take Cameron to school
- Deliver Safe Kids 101 books to the Girl Scout Council
- Back home for my breakfast
- Meet Pam at 10 a.m. for her counseling session

The day was going to be full, but organized and ordinary, just like most of my days. I'm an involved wife, mother, friend, business owner, and encourager. I like to keep my finger on the pulse of what's going on in my world. I care deeply about others, especially my family. If a person starts their day with Jesus and organization—in that order, of course—then the way is marked and things won't slip up and surprise you. Or so I thought. It just wasn't going to be that way on this rainy day. This was the day when everything in our world would change. To better understand the events of The Rainy Day better, let me back up a little. Let me tell you a bit more about our All-American family . . .

* * * * * * *

The beginning of 2004 found me living my American dream. David and I had just celebrated twenty-two years of marriage and were enjoying, to the full, our wonderful "tried and true" relationship. We had two amazing children, smart, clever, and living successful lives for their ages. Aubrey was attending Vanderbilt University on a full academic scholarship and studying biomedical engineering. She had been valedictorian of her high school class, and we were so honored to be her parents. Son Cameron, after homeschooling for five years, had just started eighth grade at David Lipscomb Middle School. We'd never considered a private Christian school for him, but after our homeschooling years it just seemed like a better option than the public schools his sister attended. He was making new friends and had come home with straight A's at Christmas break. Although the tuition stretched our budget somewhat, our plan was to trust God to provide the funds needed each year.

Our company, Smart Kids 101, had just finished its third video training curriculum, Polite Kids 101. David and I together had started our company in 1997. Our first course, *Babysitting 101*, had done well in both wholesale and retail markets. Our second video, *Safe Kids 101*, released in 2002. I was eager to get my marketing plans implemented so our newest program would be as successful as the first two. Getting the video masters ready for replication proved challenging for us; the replication company rejected the first three masters. Something about their machines being "testy."

"Pssshh. . . . So get your machines fixed," I'd mutter under my breath. Fortunately, the fourth trip to the replicators ended in success. It took a lot of perseverance from both David and myself. While the process was frustrating and hard to understand, it was simply a case of putting your head down and persevering to finish what needed to be done! No time for whining, fretting, or freaking out. Stay the course, keep your eye on the prize, and good things will come from your efforts. This was our family's standard, how we lived, communicated, and interacted with one another. While driving the master to the replicators the final time, the Holy Spirit impressed this thought on me: *Polite Kids 101 is David's gift to you.*

Yes, I thought, *my sweet husband works very hard to support our family at his day job and then helps his crazy wife with her dreams of teaching and training the kids of the world! God bless him!* The thought came again: *This is David's gift to YOU!* In a few short days, I would understand what that impression truly meant.

We lived in a condominium David had gutted and remodeled mostly by himself. It took more than four years of hard, intense work. How about hanging twenty-seven pieces of Sheetrock by yourself? David Hunt did. We called our little condo home, and it was perfect for us. David felt such accomplishment in doing the work, whether it was demolition, framing, hanging drywall, taping, mudding, painting, or installing new appliances. He did everything himself with the exception of the plumbing and electrical installation. David could do just about anything he set his mind to. If he didn't know how to do something he'd buy a book and teach himself or look it up online. His degree, from Oklahoma State University, was in radio-TV-film, and this is where we met. His first job was behind the camera and he enjoyed it, although, if needed, he could direct, produce, and write as well. He prided himself in his photojournalism skills because he was, at heart, a creator. He loved the creative process, and those he worked with and for considered him the best. He crafted with excellence, working with many influencers and celebrities of the '80s and '90s. Folks like President George H. W. Bush, Oprah Winfrey, Garth Brooks, and my favorite, Captain Kangaroo. (Yes, Captain Kangaroo!) Videos of David's sunsets (well, actually they were God's first; He gave them to David) were shown on *NBC Nightly News*. The producers of *Entertainment Tonight* nicknamed David "the human tripod" because his handheld video shots were so steady. He earned this title through shooting video on a small boat in the middle of the Caribbean. He was strong, stubborn, and really, really good at his craft.

We weren't a financially wealthy family by any stretch, but we were extremely wealthy where it mattered: We loved God and expressed unconditional love for each other every moment of every day. We had plenty to eat, a roof over our heads, clothes to wear, and treated one another with respect and honor. And we paid our bills on time every month. Yep, we pretty much covered the bases and lived life well. That was very important to David and me.

David had a great job at the Saturn Corporation in Spring Hill, Tennessee. He worked in the media department and many, many times described his work days as "being paid to play," "working with a band of brothers," or like working with college buddies. He loved his job in corporate media, which I think surprised him a little. David was a grease monkey. He found much enjoyment tinkering around in his garage. Little hobbies like pulling a V-12 engine from a 1984 Jaguar and replacing it with a V-8, 350 engine . . . believe it or not, these things relaxed him and gave him immense satisfaction. Go figure!

He was also safety guy in our family, constantly preparing us for the "what-ifs" of life. Breakdown on the road? No problem. David traveled with a toolbox that would make any paid mechanic green with envy. Electricity out? No worries. We had a full complement of flashlights, batteries, and candles organized and at our fingertips. Fire in our condo? We had two upstairs ladders and children trained and at the ready to let them down and crawl to safety. We had our family central meeting place, at the nearby Dumpster, and if we chose to "fight" instead of take flight, we even had two sizes of fire extinguishers. In short, David was a conscientious, safe man, one who took his role of protector of our family extremely seriously. We were fortunate, knowing that if we had a problem, our husband and daddy had a plan in mind and was ready to execute it at the drop of a hat.

Ask our children, even today, about tornado season when they were kids. They will tell you—now they have a gleam in their eye, recalling it—that Daddy rallied us all safely in the basement many spring evenings. "Grab your pillows, blankets, Honey Jo Bear, and whatever you want to save and get downstairs now," he directed. While it was inconvenient at the time and sometimes seemed like overkill, our sleepy heads knew it came from his heart full of love for us. I knew David's thought: *Ain't nothing gonna happen on my watch!* We respected him, even if we didn't always understand him! David was intense. But time and time again we witnessed this soft, beautiful side that made us understand, even more, his deep and abiding love for his family.

Our miniature dachshund, Gretta, brought out a side of

David that few ever saw, including the kids and me. When this little eight-pound wiener dog won him over, we didn't know whether to snicker at him and roll our eyes or clobber him over the head with her cage! We got Gretta as a sort of rescue dachshund from a good friend. David didn't think we needed a dog, especially in a condo. "It's cruel to have a dog confined all the time!" he'd snap.

But when our friend offered a free, eight-month-old dachshund that would be taken to the pound if we didn't take her in, I somehow talked him into it. The proposition didn't come without conditions, though. Here were David's stipulations:

1. We take her for the weekend first, before any decisions are made.
2. She goes back Monday morning if it doesn't work out.
3. She is only allowed on the main level of our condominium: no upstairs and no downstairs!

I'm not sure that last mandate even lasted through Sunday morning! David quickly realized what a beautiful addition Gretta was to our family, and besides, she was already ruling the roost! In that first year the man who didn't even think we needed a dog would regularly unzip his jacket, put her inside, and zip it back up. "I don't want her to be cold," he would say, a weak defense against his actions.

One winter he cut the sleeves out of an old sweatshirt and turned one of the sleeves into a sort of hoodie/sweatshirt for Gretta. He called it her "Little Joey tough-girl outfit" because she looked like a hoodlum in it. He was certainly a complicated man, and I loved him dearly.

While we lived a simple family life in a fun city and beautiful state, we also lived intentional lives with a solid foundation of Christian beliefs. As a couple, David and I loved hard and fought hard. We didn't always do marriage perfectly, but many things we did right. Living a life with no regrets was an unspoken rule in our family. We never let the sun go down on our anger. We both routinely humbled ourselves and admitted when we'd messed up. We were committed to always being together, searching for the common ground in our situation, and building from there. We never joked about living apart and the word "divorce" never crossed our lips, even as a joke. We took our marriage very seriously, probably because both of us had experienced the fallout from broken homes in our teen years. Believe me when I say some days were extremely hard and our human nature would try to get us to believe that throwing in the towel would be the easiest solution. But we never truly let ourselves go there. We were committed to getting through, and to do that meant keeping the Lord Jesus Christ front and center in our marriage. If we lived from that place of devotion to both Jesus and each other, God would bless us and we'd make it. We were committed to never becoming a divorce statistic. We were going to make it—and make it for fifty, sixty, maybe even seventy-five years if the good Lord willed!

What were those core beliefs that made our marriage so strong? We believe there is a sovereign God and that He loves us with an everlasting love. We believe He has a plan for our family and always has our best interests at heart. We also believe this for our children. The fact is, He loves them even more than we do. We surrendered, submitted, and followed that plan in radical obedience for more than twenty-two years. We set goals, prayed, and trusted God to use our family to perform His good work to completion.

It was odd—even ironic—but from the beginning of our tragic Rainy Day, I declared to myself and others that if any family was prepared for an accident or hardship, we were.

Not that we lived life expecting tragedy, but we lived each day knowing that our relationship with God was important and our relationships with one another were too. We were a praying family, a hugging family, and a family who daily told each other: "I love you!"

What I said before is worth repeating: We didn't let the sun go down on our anger, and we practiced open, transparent living—what you saw is what you got. I believe this is wisdom from the Holy Spirit, and our family was privileged to walk it out every single day.

TWO

ORDINARY, RAINY MORNING

It was an exciting time and we were celebrating! *Polite Kids 101* was finally complete and I had exactly one thousand VHS copies in my office, just waiting for customers. We'd been trying to get our product out for the last two weeks, but between tight schedules and those uncooperative replicating machines, we'd just crossed the finish line—and it felt great.

I went on to bed early after my busy Wednesday, but David stayed up to fix a shelf in our refrigerator. It had broken just after the holidays, and by the time we isolated the problem and found the part online, wouldn't you know it—it was February! It sure would be good to have another shelf available in the fridge! How I loved my little handyman!

We had a good night's sleep but woke up to pouring rain. We knew the rain was coming. The weather forecast in our area had predicted it all week. David always put the coffee on the night before and programmed it to make early in the morning. It would be ready when his early bird wife got up to fetch her worm for the day. After my quiet time, I would fill up his mug and take it to him. We had a little routine. I would clank and rattle our mugs together and announce the arrival of the coffee wagon. That was David's weekday alarm clock. I'd bring the coffee, rub his back, hug and kiss him. Gretta would wake up too—yes, she slept with us by now—and we'd talk about our day ahead for a bit, then he would shower and I'd go downstairs to walk Gretta and start breakfast.

On this rainy morning Cameron and I would say our good-byes and he would head off to school. On Thursdays I met with my moms in prayer group at the school. David would finish up his breakfast and head off to work. This rainy morning he would also take the time to email his mother. He wanted to check in with her, tell her about the heavy rains we were having, and tell her he loved her.

My prayer group was over around 8:30 a.m., and I was to meet a Girl Scout troop leader between 8:45 and 9 at the Girl Scout Council. She wanted to teach Safe Kids 101 to her Girl Scout junior troop over the weekend and needed workbooks and certificates. After that meeting, I drove home and had just enough time to eat a quick breakfast before meeting with Pam and her counselor. Pam was my dear friend in the third year of her cancer crisis. She had a wonderful husband, five children, and a stage four diagnosis. This 37-year-old woman was knitted deeply in my heart, and if I could do anything to help make life easier for her I would. She and her husband invited me to doctor appointments; I would make juices for her alternative medicine treatments. Now I was accompanying her to therapy sessions so she would have someone to process things with and make the most of each session. If you've ever seen the movie trilogy Lord of the Rings, Pam was my Samwise Gamgee and I was her Frodo Baggins. We were close friends, locked arm in arm, living out the hard places of life and encouraging each other in the love and freedom Jesus had purchased for us. I'd go to war for and with Pam, and she would do the same for me.

"What for breakfast? What for breakfast?" I asked, tapping my toe and wondering how much time I actually had to eat. I decided on peanut butter toast and hot chocolate. It was easy and offered warmth for a cold, rainy February morning. This was also my fallback comfort breakfast from childhood. I requested this breakfast when I needed extra encouragement or became a little anxious.

Makes sense to me, I told myself. I'd already had a busy morning and the therapy session would take an emotional toll on me too, even though I would never let Pam know that. She needed me and I would be there for her.

At about 10 a.m. the phone rang. It was Michael Kramer, David's boss. This was a bit unusual.

"Jules, it's Kramer. Have you heard from David?"

"No, why?"

"Well, because we think he's been in an accident."

"Oh, Kramer! Seriously? Is he all right?"

"We don't know. All we've heard is there was an accident and one person was taken to Williamson Medical Center and the other one taken to Vanderbilt. I'll find out more and call you back."

"OK. Thank you!"

As you might imagine, my head was suddenly spinning. I hung up the phone and fell to my knees. I don't remember what I prayed, but I'm sure my heavenly Father had already summoned the ministering angels to meet me there on my dining room floor. I immediately thought: *Whoever went to Vanderbilt is definitely in much worse shape than the person on their way to Williamson County.* I'm not sure how or why I knew that Vanderbilt Medical Center had the only Trauma 1 unit in our area. All critically injured patients were trans ported to that hospital if possible. People with lesser injuries, non-life threatening, were taken to the hospital nearest them. The phone rang a few minutes later, and again it was Kramer.

"Jules, David's on his way to Vanderbilt."

"I'm on my way. Thanks, Michael."

I ran through the house.

"What do I do? What do I do?" Out of nothing but instinct, I grabbed my purse, cell phone, and keys and dashed to the van.

I was suddenly talking to myself. "I need to call Pam to tell her I can't meet with her. I need to call Mom, Jim at church, Kim, and Leta. They'll call others . . . think, think, think, Julie!"

The rain was still coming down hard during my 15-minute drive up Hillsboro Road to Vanderbilt Medical Center. I needed to pay attention, stay safe, and figure out what to do next. I was like a fine-tuned instrument, a well-trained soldier in the army of God. I felt not only His presence, but also His power, within me. I knew I had to stay calm and not entertain any talk that was contrary to His Word. I called my mother. She was very upset, almost hysterical. I knew I couldn't let myself go to that level of emotion. I interrupted her. "Mom, Mom! Listen to me! We will not act like pagans in a crisis! Settle down! We are ready for whatever comes our way. We were born for such a time as this!"

I shake my head even now as I recall saying those words. I am but a woman; I've made so many mistakes in my life, walked in sin, and have made a total mess of many situations, for which I am very sorry. But one thing I do know: I had been reading and planting the Word of God deep inside my heart for many years. Daily Bible reading, praying regularly, going to church, attending Bible studies, watching Joyce Meyer on television, reading godly writers like Oswald Chambers and John Eldredge—these were all part of the good seed I had been planting inside my heart for years. It was now springing up inside me when I needed it most. This seed was now bearing full-grown plants of strength, courage, hope, and love. It was ripe and ready for the picking, and boy did I need a harvest that morning! I'm so grateful for the discipline of studying God's Word, seeking His kingdom first, and choosing right living! That is what I attribute my superwoman-type strength and presence of mind to. He is faithful. The grace is available and sufficient. Believe me, it was entirely the Holy Spirit bringing me what I needed at the moment.

I ended the call with Mom, made other calls, then started praying again for David, the kids, and me. I asked God for strength, wisdom, and comfort for all of us.

Then I pulled into the emergency room parking lot.

THREE

THE
HOSPITAL

I saw an ambulance, and two attendants were collapsing a gurney. I rolled down my window and asked if they had brought in a patient from the I-65 and Saturn Parkway area. They answered that they had, and I asked where the patient had been taken. "Through the double doors. Just leave your van here with the keys and the valet will park it for you," one of them answered.

"I'm the man's wife. How is he? Is it bad?" I inquired.

He told me that David was alert, awake, and talking; this is a good sign, he added. But he went on to say he was concerned about David's distended abdomen, which could indicate internal bleeding.

I went inside the ER, told them who I was, and they handed me what seemed to be an alarming amount of paperwork for someone in my situation. I started getting annoyed. I'm shocked, numb, upset, and just want to have a glimpse of my husband. Is he in pain, critical, just on the other side of the wall?

"Can I just see him for a minute?" I inquired. "I don't want him to die while I'm over here filling out paperwork." They assured me that I'd be able to see him as soon as he was ready, but that the doctors were working on him, trying to get him stable. I went on to finish the paperwork and took a seat on a vinyl waiting room chair. Our pastor, Jim, walked through the doors and I filled him in. Pam arrived, and I let Jim fill her in because the nurse was calling me up to the desk. My heart leaped at the thought of finally getting to see my sweet David.

"We forgot to take his wedding band off when we were locking up his personal belongings," she said when I reached the desk. "We can't open the security boxes once we close them. Can we just give the ring to you and let you hang onto it? You are his wife, right?"

"Yes, I am," I proudly answered. "Can I see him yet?"

"No, not yet. But we'll let you know as soon as you can, honey."

I put David's gold wedding band on my thumb. I liked having it that close to me, to look at it and nervously twist it around when I didn't know what else to do. Waiting in the sterile hospital emergency room lobby with Jim and Pam was excruciating. I wanted to know more about his condition so badly, but no one was telling me anything. By this time Stephan, David's good friend from work, and the youth group leaders from our church had arrived. Paige, a friend from church and a Vanderbilt University Medical Center employee, just happened into the ER the same time we were there. When she saw Pastor Jim, she knew something was up and headed over. Then, she saw me.

"Oh Julie, what's happened?" I filled her in and she assured me she would call her mama and together they would "get the prayer chain going." I graciously thanked her because I knew

I was starting to run low on hope.

The doctor came out while a test was being run on David; he talked with me about his condition. This was the first information after what already seemed like a forever-wait. Pastor Jim was in the room with me, and I don't know if the doctor was a poor communicator or I was a poor listener, because my head was spinning so fast. I remember thinking, *Good Lord, can this doctor just get to the point?*

I like to give and receive direct communication, and this doctor wasn't cutting it. *Hopefully,* I thought, *Jim is listening well, because I can't follow the man at all.* I decided to use my journalistic training to ask a few probing questions.

"What are you saying? Is David in serious condition?"

"He's got a lot going on. Do you have family in town?" he asked.

"No, just our kids." I answered.

"How old are they? Like, older?"

This seemed, to me, like a strange way to phrase a question. I was trying to process this conversation, and it was not at all going like I imagined it would.

"Yes, our daughter goes to school here at Vanderbilt, and our son is at David Lipscomb Middle School."

By now I was working *really* hard to stay calm. It would've been much easier to scream and throw myself on the floor in a fit! But, in reality, what would that have helped? Not much. Hysterical women rarely get positive attention. Besides, according to the Bible, God has given me *everything* I need for life and godliness. That means He's already provided self-control and peace for me. I just needed to dip my hand into His soothing, unending well and help myself.

"You should get your children here. If his parents or siblings are close, you should call them and tell them to come," he calmly answered. This doctor was working very hard, it was becoming obvious to me, to recall his memorized script of how to handle communicating with a family in this sort of crisis.

"They all live out of state, like Tulsa and in Texas!" I answered.

I was starting to have the picture drawn for me, and it was not a good one. I wished with all my heart I had just been sucked into a television drama: *Playing the role of the distressed, but calm, wife is Julie Hunt.* But this was no television drama. This was my life, this was my husband, and I was starting to get really, really scared. I summoned every ounce of courage within my being and asked the doctor as calmly as I could, "So, what are you trying to say? Could David die?" My lip quivered while I waited for his answer. I looked at Jim and looked back at the doctor.

"Yes, it is possible. He's seriously injured. There's a bleeding issue, and if we don't find out where it is and get it stopped, he may not survive."

This trained reporter needed no further questions or answers. I got it. I didn't like it, but I got it. I turned to Jim and asked him to go get Cameron at the middle school.

"Do not, I repeat, do not let them tell him anything. You don't tell the school anything in advance. I will not have Cameron hear this from anyone but you, Jim."

I was in full mother bear-protecting mode. My cubs were in danger. An emotional jab was coming that could wipe them out, and I intended to shield them as much as possible, even if it meant stepping in front and taking the blow myself.

Jim nodded and told me he understood. He left while Pam, Stephan, and I headed up to the tenth floor critical care unit where David was headed after his test.

My next mission was our daughter, Aubrey. Her cell phone was off because she was in class that morning. We kept calling. I knew at some point she'd turn her phone back on and either answer it or see the crazy number of missed calls from her mom and others. I thanked God silently that she was right here on the Vanderbilt campus. This beautiful, bright, intelligent daughter could have gone to college anywhere—and I mean anywhere—she wanted to go. But two years earlier, God placed on her heart: "Vanderbilt University. I'll make a way for you to go to Vanderbilt University." And she didn't want to go anywhere else. Our loving, kind, caring Father has the big picture of our lives in focus. He knows what's going to happen, and when we let go and trust Him, He directs our steps in unbelievably precise detail. My daughter was but ten minutes away at the most critical time of our lives, of her life. That was nothing short of a divinely inspired God-moment. How I praise Him! No other deities do this for their followers. There is no one like our God—even when we're living our worst nightmare, He is with us, making a way!

* * * * * *

It was about an hour later when I got to see David for the first time. He was sedated, a tube down his throat, and on his way to an angiogram. They still hadn't found the source of his severe bleeding they were desperately trying to locate. David couldn't talk to me, but he tried. His muddled noises were inaudible. Oh, how I wished he could've said something, anything, to me! I was feeling desperate when I realized maybe he could hear me! I leaned in. "Cooter, it's your woman. We are all here praying and fighting for you. I love you, honey. Be strong. We're all here. Get out your sword and fight too. We're here, honey."

An unfocused glance was all that he could give. He tried to speak, and obviously couldn't. There was a tube down his throat. I told him to not try to speak. I just wanted him to know that we were all there with him and loved him very much.

Of course, I had no way to realize at this moment just what the Rainy Day was bringing to our family. I didn't know much about what was happening with David and I didn't know when the nightmare would end. But what I did know was that our little family was receiving an outpouring of love from friends coming to the hospital to show support and pray with us. Church and school friends, longtime friends, and folks who barely knew us came to say, "We care and we're praying." It meant so much to me.

Two in particular were such sweet gestures. My high school friend, Carol Oxford Edwards, came to the hospital. I hadn't seen her in years, even though we live in the same area of Middle Tennessee. But when my mom, in Davis, Oklahoma, called her church's prayer chain, Carol's mom got a call and then called Carol. She told her mom, "I'm embarrassed that I haven't seen Julie in years and we live in the same town. But I want to go to the hospital." When I saw Carol's face, a friend from childhood, my hometown, my heart was so comforted. I knew God was comforting my confused and aching heart.

Another precious visit was the middle school secretary at Cameron's school. My fogged-in mind introduced her to others as "Miss Judy, Cameron's secretary." We all got a quick chuckle because it sounded like Cameron had his own administrative assistant in eighth grade! Of course, knowing Cameron, it wouldn't surprise us! But it did give us some wonderful comic relief for a few seconds.

I don't really remember much about Aubrey getting there. I think I talked briefly with her while she was walking over from campus. She had just gotten off the phone with her boyfriend of four years. He went to college at Tennessee Tech University, which is about two hours east of Nashville. His mother had called him as soon as she heard from our church family that David had been in a serious car accident. He dropped everything and drove straight to the hospital. He was at the hospital before Aubrey even got out of class, which means he was there to support her as soon as she found out her daddy was in critical condition.

I waited with our children and friends and nervously twirled on my thumb, around and around, the strongest physical connection between my heart and David's: that gold wedding band.

FOUR

SAYING
GOOD-BYE

Things began moving so quickly that it's really hard to recall much with great detail. I remember the ICU waiting room was filled to capacity with our friends. One of the nurses requested that all but ten of our visitors go down to the second-floor waiting area. Folks were reluctant, but they followed the hospital's rules. A small group of us—our kids, our pastor Casey, and a couple of prayer warriors from church—were moved to a tiny waiting room closer to the area where David was. We were told that when David could have visitors we'd be taken to see him. That wait took forever. I prayed and kept still before the Lord. I have never prayed so hard and believed so strongly for a miracle; that's exactly what we needed, and we needed it soon.

Around 1:30 p.m., Aubrey, Cameron, and I were allowed to go back to the critical care unit. Unfortunately, the nurse designated to lead us back to the CCICU didn't show much sympathy, which added to my anxiety.

After we were scrubbed, we proceeded to David's bed. There were beeping machines and medical staff scurrying all around him. Nurses had charts, recording numbers that were shouted from across the room. Other nurses performed tests while still others heard the numbers and would fling a bag of something across the room so it could be hooked to David's IV. I was distracted but tried to listen to the nurse's assessment of the situation.

"He's very critical, but we're doing all we can for him. If he makes it the next few hours, then we'll try to get him through to 24 hours, then 48, then 72. If he makes it till then, we'll try to get him through a week, two, three weeks. You all have a very long road ahead of you. If he survives, he'll be in the hospital at least for three months, then rehab for another six months, then home recovery. If he survives, you're looking at maybe two years until things are looking like normal again. His injuries are quite significant."

I tried to follow what the nurse was saying. My head was still spinning and the words were going around and around with concepts and madness that wouldn't take hold in my brain. But I do remember praying under my breath: "God, I will stay with this man for the rest of my life, caring for him, no matter the cost. I'll nurse him back to health, we'll get permission to build a wheelchair ramp at the condo, and I will see that David is well and loved, because I know You will help me, God." It's funny where the mind goes in situations it cannot agree with. I never saw this as the end of the road for David. I only saw it as an unexpected twist in the journey. The nurse told us we could talk to David, tell him whatever we wanted to say. Even though he couldn't respond in his drug-induced coma, he could hear us. I'm not sure what the kids told him, but I told him we were praying for him, our friends had gathered at the hospital, and his mom was getting a flight out of

Tulsa soon. I told him I loved him very, very much.

About seven minutes had passed since we made the journey down the hallway to see him. The male nurse interrupted my conversation with David and asked, "Did you hear those numbers? It's not getting better, and we need for you to leave now." We all took one last look at him and turned to start down the hallway, back to the small waiting room that had, for that day, become our altar to the Most High.

God is faithful to bring you the people you need most at the critical moments in life.

Believers are His hands and feet, and I needed to know folks were praying. I witnessed this as the forty or so people gathered at the hospital grew—seemingly exponentially— to hundreds as word spread through the afternoon. Prayer chains were initiated; office workers paused to lift David and our little family to the throne room of God. At our son's school, students were praying and trying to figure out ways to help. Beauty was kindled in the hearts of people who love and care. If you are reading this and were part of that rainy day in 2004, consider yourself hugged in the most heartfelt fashion and thanked beyond words. I truly believe you were part of God's plan for us that day, and you made a difference.

Folks in the small room prayed, and the kids and I listened and agreed while our bodies and minds went numb. In moments like these, it's much easier to rest in that state rather than remain in the present. It's a hard moment, unsettling, yet peaceful. It's a moment where the Holy Spirit will break through in the hardest, most comforting ways, if you let Him. Cameron picked up the Bible and started reading the psalms. He elbowed me and pointed at a page. "I just stumbled onto this," he said in a low, hushed voice. As soon as I read it, my heart shifted. Our beautiful Savior, who loves us, takes care of us in the most precious and detailed ways. He sent a message to our son through His Word, a message that would give us a glimpse into the next season of life: Psalm 146. Cameron read the whole thing, but when he elbowed me, he pointed to verse 9: "The Lord watches over the alien and sustains the fatherless and the widow, but He frustrates the ways of the wicked."

I looked at him with a heavy and questioning heart. "Cameron, what are you saying?"

"No matter what happens, Mom, God will take care of us," my 14-year-old man-child declared with authority.

This is the Trinity: Father, Son, and Holy Spirit, working together to make sure it is well with our souls.

Jesus says in John 14:16-18:

And I will ask the Father, and He will give you
another advocate to help you and be with you forever—
The Spirit of truth. The world cannot accept Him,
because it neither sees Him nor knows Him. But you know
Him, for He lives with you and will be in you.
I will not leave you as orphans; I will come to you.

A loving, tender, and merciful Father provides, and in moments like these, He allows us to experience peace. He gave His only Son to be my Savior. To save me from my sin that would eventually kill me and sentence me to a life apart from Him. He sent His Spirit to comfort me in moments like these, to lift my gaze off of those beige hospital walls and up to His, His loving eyes of favor. He loves me. He created me for fellowship with Him. He wants me; God misses me when I run away from Him or when I don't take our relationship as seriously as He does. I remember thinking: *My Father is with me in this small, makeshift prayer room.* He is with our daughter, Aubrey, holding her heart, sheltering her from the pounding "what-ifs" that are bombarding her thoughts. And He is with our son, Cameron, giving him practical words from His Word. And I am a mother, speechless, as I feel comfort within the raging battle that is called my life. I trust. I trust that what my son has mined out of Scripture is from the Spirit of truth that lives within me, and I am comforted, if only for a moment. I'll take it.

And now the door opens, and it's the doctor. He tells me they've done an extremely radical, invasive operation for David. I twirl the gold band faster and faster as I listen.

"We have split him open, from sternum to pubic bone. We've pulled his internal organs out to give his lungs space to expand with breath. It's our last-ditch effort. We haven't been successful in stopping the internal bleeding. We are giving him blood, plasma, as fast as we can, but he just bleeds out. I'm very sorry, but we are in an extremely grave situation." Seconds pass and the door opens again. A nurse says, "He's coding." The doctor turns to me. "You must come with me right away. Leave your children here."

We run down the hall. A nurse leads me straight into David's room. I am not prepared for what I have stumbled into. David's bed must have fifteen medical personnel around it. It is loud. Some are counting, some are announcing technical information, and one person is on top of David's chest, straddled, doing manual chest compressions with great physical exertion. There is so much commotion around me, but the nurse knows exactly what to do. She takes my hand and leads me straight to David's side. She tells me: "Grab his hand and talk to him now! He can hear every word you say, so tell him everything you want him to know now!"

I begin . . .

"David, I love you so much. But listen to me now. You've got to fight with everything you've got to win this battle. David, take out your sword and swing it, honey! Don't give in; you've got to fight, fight hard. Come on, David. I know you are strong and God is for us! David, David, David, I love you, I'm here for you, we'll get through this, I know we will." I stop to wipe the tears and catch my breath. I look straight at him, his broken body, wrapped tightly with surgical gauze. His face is bruised and swollen with tubes coming from seemingly everywhere. The tiny cuts from the car window glass that shattered into a million jagged pieces. The horseshoe-shaped gash on top of his head, where his jet-black hair met the hard windshield on impact . . . and my world now spins in slow motion, and then time freezes. . . . I bend down to my beloved and whisper: "Precious, sweet David. If what you are experiencing right now is something that I cannot see or appreciate, if what you know to be true right now is something I can't even imagine, then I trust you to go, Sweetie. Go if you have to go. I love you and I trust you." As I finish my sentence, my eyes are drawn to the gold wedding band around my thumb, and then the most miraculous thing happens. I feel, and *see*, a squeeze! David, at that very moment, squeezes my hand, and my heart skips a beat. I turn to the nurse, whose hand rests around my waist. "He heard me, he squeezed my hand. He's fighting!" I exclaim.

And then, suddenly, I hear a strange voice in the room. "Call it." It is the medic on top of David's chest.

I look at David. I hear a long tone and the nurse with her arm around my waist says, "I'm sorry, honey. He's gone." Without missing a beat, I whisper to her, "Are you a Christian?" She answers, "Yes, I am."

"Well, I don't want to be weird," I continue, "but I want you to get my two pastors and my children in the waiting area and bring them back here to me."

"Sure, I can do that," she says.

I went on. "Well, I want to ask God to raise him from the dead, just like the New Testament says we can do."

And she answers, so sweetly, "OK, sure."

I look at David's body. It sure has taken a beating. I hurt because I know how much he hurt. Our two pastors, with Aubrey and Cameron, walk in. The medical team is cleaning up and shutting everything down. They pull the curtains around us, on all four sides, for our privacy. I look at my kids and tell them, "Daddy's gone, but I want us to pray and ask God if He wants to raise Daddy back to life." They know the Word of God and understand that this is God's decision, but that it is our obedience to His Word to ask Him for a miracle.

I have no idea what to say or do, I just know that I'd read in the Bible that believers are able to do this, and I at least want to give God the opportunity. So that's what we do. For seven minutes or so, we each lay our hands on David and pray. The kids and I lay our bodies across David and ask God to breathe life back into him. I remember looking out across the skyline of Nashville from the tenth-floor CCICU, inviting God to revive David's body and bring a miracle of the dead, raising him right there in Nashville, Tennessee. I give Him an open invitation from our family to do whatever He wants to do . . . and we wait. I'm not sure how long, but it was ample time for the Creator-God to do His will for David, for us.

At what seems like the right moment, I look at our pastor and ask, "It's just David's time to go, isn't it?" He shakes his head and says, "Yes, Julie, I think it is."

I turn to the kids. "Daddy will never be warmer than he is right now, so love on him, talk to him, hug him, kiss him, do whatever you need to do. Now's the time."

These may be the hardest words for a mom to say to her children, but believe me, it's even harder to watch. I've been through many hard, unimaginably difficult places, but this was the worst I'd known. To witness our children drape themselves around their father's lifeless body and beg God to let him come back to us was almost too much for a person to bear. They cried, they moaned, they prayed . . . and you know what? God heard it all and was there with us. He held our breaking hearts and kept them from shattering. He pushed our tear-soaked bangs away from our faces and dried our eyes. He let us fall in His arms and sob and sob and sob.

He was there, comforting us, just like He promised He would.

Blessed are those who mourn, for they will be comforted (Matthew 5:4).

We walk out to thirty or so friends who line the hallway of the critical care unit. The expressions of sorrow and anguish on their faces actually bring comfort to my plunged-in-sorrow heart.

I know they understand. I know we aren't alone. I know God is making a way for us.

FIVE

THE UNKNOWN PATH

Everyone relocated to the first floor chapel just to be together for a while. I felt like I'd been to war, and I'm sure the others felt the same. By this time our senior pastor, Steve Fry, had come to the hospital and offered to lead us in praise and worship if we wished to do so. I truly couldn't think of any place I'd rather be than in the throne room of my Jesus, sitting at His feet. I was reminded of John 6:61. When many were deserting Jesus, He asked His disciples: "Do you want to leave too?" Peter answered, "Lord, to whom shall we go? You have the words of eternal life."

That's how I felt. I had to go and worship my Father, receiving comfort from His Holy Spirit—because I knew I didn't have anywhere else to go.

So we sang. We poured out our hearts in worship to the only One who understands. We cried, rejoiced, and gave God all the honor and glory He is so worthy of.

Cameron had a word rise up in him, and how I wish now we'd had a way to record it. This kid—really, my young man—basically started preaching the Word of God to gathered friends. His text was right out of the book of Job. His context was simple: God is good all the time, and all the time, God is good. He declared that we would miss Dad, but we were trusting God and God is bigger. My son, processing all of this with such depth and maturity! It was incredible, and certainly it was the power of God rising up to comfort, encourage, and support our breaking hearts.

Our worship and Word lasted about an hour. We were exhausted and needed to get home. Our good friends Bob and Suzanne Rannells drove my van back to the condo, transporting both Aubrey and me. Cameron got a ride home with a friend. We were mostly quiet on the fifteen-minute drive. It's funny what will pop into a person's mind in times like these. During the trip home, I thought: *Oh wow. David won't have a video of his life at the service. How sad that the person who's made sure everyone else has his or her great video moment won't have a great video moment of his own. Oh well. I have more than that to worry about now, so I won't think about that anymore.* And you know what? I didn't.

And somewhat unbelievably, it was *still* raining all the way home. What a messy, messy day. We pulled the van into the garage, and I could tell people were already inside. I had given my key to Pam earlier in the day so she could come home and walk Gretta for me. I came up the stairs to the sweetest sight. The lights were on, candles were lit, music was softly playing, and many friends were in the kitchen. There was a spread of food on the center island like I couldn't believe. Sandwich meats, cheeses, bread, chips, pickles, cookies, on and on. I shook my head in amazement. "This is what church ladies do, ya'll. You sure got it right! Thank you."

"Let us fix you something to eat, Julie," someone coaxed.

"I'm sorry. Thank you. But I'm just not hungry right now," I said softly.

"We understand. How about something to drink then? We've got Diet Coke?"

"That would be great," I answered.

I walk into my living room and sink into the couch. I'm numb. I don't feel anything. I know I'm supposed to feel something, but I don't. I don't care about anything. I don't know where my children are. I'm suspended in air and moving in slow motion. I'm occupying a body, but I don't feel alive. It's the strangest feeling. I don't know what to do. I should be doing something, but I don't know what. I guess I need to start letting people know. *Who are they? Who out there needs to know what's happened today? Who are the people who need to know David's gone?*

Folks have been so kind to keep our extended family posted several times throughout the day. I remember my friend Pam just taking my phone and calling my mom, sister, and others because she knew I could not. I was told that David's mom was on her way from Tulsa and would land in a couple of hours, around 10:30 p.m. A wave of sorrow swept through me. *What am I going to say to her? How can I even look her in the eye and connect her with the reality?* "Your David is gone. The one you birthed, loved, cared for, scraped knees and all, who you encouraged during Mighty Might Football. He doesn't live anymore."

And suddenly, I can't cope with the thought. I can't breathe. I run outside in the rain. I remember: our neighbors. All of our neighbors need to know. Our little mailbox where we'd see each other, check in, and make sure everybody was OK was now forever changed. *We're not OK . . . no, we're certainly not OK. Something terrible has happened today.* David and I would no longer be known to the single, career-minded young adults on our street as the only married couple with kids. Now I'm the one whose husband died, the widow with those poor children. *Really, God? Really? This is my new title—widow? I don't think I want this, God. You didn't even ask me if I'd be OK with this! Well, I'm not! I'm not OK!* I'm in the dark, standing in the rain! I shouldn't be outside in the rain by myself! I manage to pull my scattered thoughts together and head back inside; a friend comes over to me.

"Your sister's on the phone, Julie. Can you talk to her?"

Of course I want to talk with Cindy, my big sis. We are so close, and she knows how to make everything right in my world. She's always been the voice of reason, my champion, my friend.

"Hey, Sis." I speak softly.

"Bee, I just called to say that Chuck and I got our flights and we'll be getting in to Nashville tomorrow night. Are you OK? How are you, sweet sister? I think Mom is flying in tomorrow too. Do you know when Russ and Jone and their boys are coming in?"

I'm robotic, repeating information someone must have told me, going through the motions.

"Yes, Mom is coming tomorrow night. I'm pretty sure that's right. I don't know about Rusty's family. You probably know more than me right now, Sis. Oh, David's mom, Dorothy, she's on her way right now. She lands at 10:30 tonight. Cindy, pray for me. This is so very hard." My voice shakes and fades away as I fight back the tears.

"Oh sweetie, I have been praying all day and my team at work has been too. What about David's sister, Mary? She knows, right?"

I explain that Mary was on a mission trip to the Bahamas and couldn't be contacted. She had eventually gotten word to call home and her husband, Mark, had to tell her the awful news. But God is so good to His children. Friends, her pastor, and fellow missionaries with her immediately prayed and loved her with God's comfort. She was to board a charter flight home the next day.

Oh, the incredible pain of it all. So very much pain. *How will God ever be able to sort through all this pain and all of these broken hearts?* This is what's running through my mind.

My mind drifts back to the conversation with my sister.

"Well, I said it earlier, but sweetie, I just want you to know that we're so sorry and we love you very much." Her heart was breaking for her little sister and her niece and nephew. Her heart was breaking for David. She loved him so much. They had a special connection: senior class of 1975, they'd say. Although they didn't go to the same high school, they did always have a special connection, a sort of "I get you" relationship.

I put the phone down and sit on the couch. Voices, music, and conversations fill the air, but I can't really hear any of it. It just doesn't matter. Nothing really matters.

Where's Cameron? I hadn't even checked on our son in the last three hours! *What is wrong with me?*

"He's upstairs in his room, Julie," someone said. "Some friends from school came over, and I think they're playing video games."

"Did he eat?" It's all I can think to offer.

"Yes, they all fixed food and took it upstairs."

I remember feeling extremely grateful that others were in my village to help me figure all this out. Before long it was time to get David's mom at the airport, and the Rannells were going to drive our van and take whoever wanted to go. There was some discussion on whether I should go. Honestly, wild horses couldn't have kept me from going, and Aubrey felt the same way. I've always been very close to Dorothy. We talked on the phone often, she treated me like another daughter, and she was very much like a second mom to me. Mimi Dorothy even lived with us and kept Aubrey when she was a baby.

They've always had a special relationship.

* * * * * * *

We met Dorothy at the airport and we all wept together. I couldn't imagine going through that first week without her. It was only right that the two women who loved David the most, his mother and his wife, face this hard road together.

Back at the condo, Aubrey helped Mimi Dorothy get settled in, and I sat staring into space in the living room. Thoughts were racing through my head. All the questions, statements, that unprepared feeling when you should know what to do, but don't, or you're in front of the class, unprepared, with no pants on. *I don't know. I just don't know how to do this part of life. It sucks. I'm tired. No, I'm exhausted.*

Oh, how I dread going upstairs to our bedroom. What am I going to do? How am I ever going to do this? Why did today, this very Rainy Day, ever have to happen?

SIX

WANDERING IN DREAMLAND

Although I was exhausted, sleep wasn't as elusive as I thought it might be. I only woke up once through that first night. Thank God. Aubrey decided to sleep over with me, and I was so glad she did. The bed didn't seem so empty, and I have a sneaking suspicion that maybe Aubrey didn't want to be alone in her dorm room either.

As much as I was hurting, I couldn't allow myself to think about what this devastation was doing to our children. No, I couldn't think about it, for fear I might never regain peace again. Grief puts the mind in such a fragile place. It feels like being on the edge of a great cliff, mostly teetering to the point that one false move, or a sigh, or a leaning in the wrong direction and . . . *woosh!* You're gone, fallen, it's over, never to return to sanity or reality again. Just gone.

When I did wake up that first night, it was particularly disturbing. Aubrey was awake too, and we talked briefly.

"You awake, sweetie?" I whispered.

"Yeah, I'm awake. You OK?" she whispered back.

"Well, I'm not sure." My voice was shaky as I fought back the tears. I think it was just hitting me really hard what had happened the day before. Maybe it was the first time I'd actually slowed my brain enough to catch up with the events of the Rainy Day.

"I'm not sure I can do this, sweetie. I'm just devastated, and I know you are too. Aubrey, sweetheart, how will we ever go on without Daddy? I don't know how. I'm just so lost."

Maybe I should have shielded her more and not been so honest about my feelings. Maybe I should've put up a stronger front and found a way to reflect a more "together" version of myself. The mom Aubrey knows and loves, the protector, should be here! The self-assured, courageous, formidable, strength-personified mom should be here. Perhaps that would've been better for her, paying more attention to her feelings of loss and what the Rainy Day had taken from her and her brother. I don't know. I just don't know.

I asked Aubrey to wake up our friend Vickie so she could pray for us. Sweet Vickie was Aubrey's boyfriend's mother. She offered to spend the night at our condominium just in case we needed someone in the night. And guess what? We did. I was so grateful to have her with us. While disrupting her sleep was the last thing I wanted to do, I knew I'd be foolish to think I could manage this night alone. I needed her, and so did my daughter. We weren't alone, so I didn't need to act like we were. She came to the bedroom and prayed the sweetest prayer for us. The Comforter came and we dozed off, back to sleep until morning.

At morning light, Vickie's night shift ended and my friend Leta came with breakfast. We've been friends for years, and if there's one thing I know about Leta, it's that she's really good at showing love through practical acts of kindness. If you've had a baby, she's there with dinner. If you need a ride to the doctor, just tell her when the appointment is. Need someone to watch your kids? Call Leta. See what I mean? She asked if I wanted coffee and, of course, I answered yes. I really enjoy coffee. David and I split a pot every morning. We even got a new coffeemaker for a Christmas present to each other. It would grind the beans and brew the coffee. It was fancy and we loved it. Coffee was definitely one of our things.

Who will I drink coffee with now?, I wondered to myself. It's funny how these little routines of life kept creeping into my thoughts. No matter how unwelcome these reminders of our life from before were, they just kept coming. . . . Leta served us, then went on with her day, and Dorothy was awake soon after and came downstairs. I offered freshly brewed coffee and the breakfast treats Leta had brought.

Since both kids were still asleep, it was a good time for Dorothy and me to talk. It was important for her to hear the details of the Rainy Day, and it was important for me to recount it. I wanted her to know all the particulars of David's last moments on earth. After all, this was her little boy. She needed to know and wanted to know. She told me he'd emailed her yesterday morning. I was thrilled he'd taken time to contact her!

"He talked about the rain, how much you'd had and how much was still coming. It was a lot of rain," she recalled as she teared up. I was in awe, once again, of a tender, divine moment. It was one of those moments where such incredible pain is met with such amazing love. How many mornings had passed where David didn't take the time to email his mom. But yesterday morning he took the time, and Dorothy now has this precious memory of how her son reached out to her for the last time.

A knock came at the door. I opened it, and there was David's good friend, Danny Petraitis. He was standing in the doorway, tears streaming down his cheeks, sobbing between his words.

"Julie, is it true? Is it true? No, no! Tell me it's not! Andy just called and . . . and he . . . he just told me David's gone!" My face answered Danny's questions. One look at me and he knew it was true. Morning eyes can be puffy, but nothing like I was sporting that morning. I asked him in and he sat with Dorothy and me for a while. We laughed, cried, and were comforted by the memories he shared with us. They were such good memories of David and Danny working together on television shows. They had been to Russia together the previous year. "We had some great times and got some great footage. David is very talented. A real master of his craft."

Danny shared that Andy told him David was the first to show him you could be a Christian and work in the television industry. "David didn't preach, but professed his faith in his everyday actions—even at work," Danny said. I liked hearing Danny's stories, and I know Dorothy did too. They made it seem like David was close. I needed to feel he was nearby.

Danny left and Gina came. My friend Gina has a very special place in my heart. She peeked around the staircase, caught my eye, and walked in with the biggest pack of toilet paper I'd ever seen! I laughed as I got up to hug her neck. It was so good to see her. Gina has a way about her that I'm so fond of. She's a friend who challenges me to keep reaching higher and deeper with God. When we have one of our marathon-long talks, you can bet it sparks good stuff! She knows our heavenly Father, and I mean *knows* Him. Her prayers take you straight to the throne room of God. She shares with such grace; it is a comforting gift so many need.

* * * * * *

Gina left after a short visit and, to be completely honest, I'm not sure about the rest of the day or evening. It all kind of runs together. It's funny how the world stops when someone you love is not in it anymore. It's hard to explain, but maybe as I keep telling my story, it will become clearer to me.

SEVEN

INDECISION

Vanderbilt Medical Center called twice to talk to me about releasing David's body. I didn't take the calls. Isn't that silly? I mean, who wants to have that conversation? Making decisions about releasing a body, where it goes next, what kind of service. *Oh my Lord!* To me, in my numbed mind, having those kinds of conversations was a terrible idea! To have this conversation within twenty-four hours of the accident felt like I was agreeing with what had happened. Well, I didn't agree with it!

I didn't want to make decisions about something I didn't even want to be happening. I wanted to ignore it—seriously! My hope was to just pass out and wake up to reclaim the beautiful life I had been living the day before yesterday, the Rainy Day. Yeah, I'd like to go back to the sunny day! The day I was happy. The *normal* day, where I kissed my husband and loved my children. The day I cooked meals, ran errands, and laughed with friends. I wanted to go back to that day. *I don't want this day or any of its nonsense.* Once again, I was teetering on the edge, irrational, ignoring today's life-realities, in the hope that it would all go away.

I stayed there for as long as I could, until Pastor Jim came over and gently asked, "Julie, can we talk about something?" The way he phrased it was so kind, so tender, and even generous. He didn't come across heavy-handed, like, "Stop playing around here! You've got decisions to make! Important people need to know what you want to do with David's body, and you're making everyone wait on you, and that's not right!"

No, he didn't do that, and it wasn't his tone; not even one chastising hint was in his voice. You see, Pastor Jim had been in the front of the battle lines with me yesterday. He saw, firsthand, what war we were in. Truth be known, he was probably carrying a few wounds himself, although he would've never let on. Jim is a pastor with a huge pastor's heart! What a combination! You'd think that's common, but I'm finding it isn't always the case.

"Hey, you doing OK?" he asked shortly after arriving.

"Whew," was all I could initially get out. I started to tear up. Less than twenty-four hours ago we were still fighting for David's life, not giving up. We were still believing for a miracle.

"It's OK. You don't have to answer." He said it all so softly.

It's so common to ask that question in most greetings, from formal to informal . . . "How are you doing?" "How's it going?" "What's up?" "Are you doing OK?" These seem like such simple questions, good icebreakers, but in this situation, they're not. In many cases, folks who ask these questions don't really want the answers; they just don't know what else to say. Hearing the truth in these situations can be very uncomfortable, especially for the one living it. Answers swing from the polite, yet guarded, "I'm fine," to the angry yet more genuine response: "How do you *think* I'm doing? I'm absolutely undone. And how are you?" Moments like these are so difficult to navigate.

Jim is different, or maybe it's just that I know his heart. I knew he would walk into the valley of the shadow of death with me. He'd proved it yesterday. I trusted him. It's so important for the grieving heart to find a person to trust. A family member, a good friend, or in my case, my pastor filling in until my family arrived.

So anyway, Jim explained that it was all a matter of simple logistics: Vanderbilt has a body and they don't like to keep bodies for long. The autopsy was completed, and it needed to be released. He asked me about my reservations; was it just difficult deciding such things, or did it feel like I was finalizing David's death? *Bingo! That was it!* It felt like if we could just keep David there, in the hospital, it would be easier to rewind the huge hands on the clock and we could just go back and fix all that went horribly wrong yesterday. I know it's silly, irrational, and even absurd. But that is what grief does to the mind and heart. The closest connections to the dearly departed one—the spouse, the parents, the children, the brother or sister, all of these dear ones—are not thinking as clearly as they were before the loss. Folks on the outer layers of grief would do well to remember this and extend kindness, help, sympathy, and support.

My logical self finally saw that there was a blip on the radar of my mind, and I could see it wasn't me making a decision for David's death. It was simply the decision about where his body would go next. All the hospital needed to transport him was the address.

Jim suggested a small, family-owned funeral home where David would be kept safe until I was ready to move forward. That suggestion was a gift from God. I wasn't ready to do anything. I didn't want to move forward. I wanted to move backward. But God spoke through Jim, and that was what I needed to help me move toward the goal, taking, at least for now, the smallest of baby steps.

This is key when dealing with the bereaved. Normal, unstressed brains are able to make quick decisions with little thought or able to process and think through a decision-making process. A traumatized brain gets stuck easily, making comprehension difficult, and the result is lost focus. I can't emphasize this enough: be gentle and loving with your hurting one. Realize the trauma they're suffering and don't push too hard, even if it means things don't get done. It's OK. I also learned during this time that the friends and family that I had strong connections with *before* the accident had earned the access, right, and privilege to speak into situations I was facing *after* the accident. I'd already invested many years in building trust and relationships that were needed in such a time as this. I was really thankful, looking back, that I had developed those relationships before the Rainy Day came.

I gave Jim the authority to call Vanderbilt and speak on my behalf. He gave them the information they needed, then handed the phone to me so I could confirm what he had requested. Jim asked if he could come back later in the afternoon to talk about arrangements. I knew it had to be done, so I said, "Yes. I'll see you later."

The rest of the day is a blur. I'm not sure what I did or how I did it. My kids were around; son Cameron mostly stayed in his room and played video games with friends from school and church. The only time I saw them was when they came out for food. Seems pretty typical for teenage boys. I just went with it and let him decompress the way he needed. We'd been through so much just a day earlier. There'd be plenty of time, a whole lifetime to talk, process, counsel, and work through what had happened.

I remember that Aubrey rarely left my side for most of the day. She was so strong and supportive, even though her own heart was completely broken. She was extremely close to her daddy. They are very much alike: smart, strong, determined, opinionated, and capable. I remember her lingering around my left side with her head on my shoulder and arm around my waist, whispering in my ear, "You're making good decisions, Mom," or "That's exactly what Daddy would've wanted." This was another special gift from God to me. I trusted and valued her opinion so deeply. I felt so unequipped to make the decisions that needed to be made straightaway. For the last twenty-two years of my life I had depended on my husband to either make decisions for our family or talk me through the best options when I had decisions to make. So much thinking and planning about afterlife decisions that should've already been discussed, before the Rainy Day—not *after* it had already crashed into our lives!

It's just proof that everyone should talk about the wishes of their loved ones and all the afterlife decisions *before* the unthinkable occurs. I'm a planner. I like lists, proposals, strategies, and action points. Because I'd been through so many losses of life, actually running point during some of those hard times, I knew the importance of planning ahead and how it eases the implementation for those left behind. But you have to have a willing participant in these conversations, and unfortunately, David didn't want to discuss such plans with me.

"That's too creepy," he'd say. Or, "We'll talk about it later, someday." But that talk never happened.

The traumatized brain does silly things. Although I felt confused and indecisive, I remember feeling a little justified, almost confident in the decisions I was forced to make now, somehow thinking, *Well, if he wouldn't tell me what he wanted while he was still alive, he'll just have to be satisfied with what he's getting, because he sure ain't coming back to tell me what to do now!*

Looking back, that might have been a bit of anger escaping, stage two of Elisabeth Kübler-Ross's famous five stages of grief, known by the acronym DABDA: Denial, Anger, Bargaining, Depression, Acceptance.[1] I tended to jump back and forth between denial and anger for quite some time, and this is quite common, by the way. David was such a strong personality. He was easy to admire, appreciate, and, as many coworkers acknowledged at his visitation, highly esteemed. He was also headstrong, opinionated, and determined. I got dizzy many times throughout our twenty-two-year marriage, swinging back and forth between "God, I love this man so much," to "I want to strangle this bullheaded husband of mine!"

David knew it too. He was well acquainted with both sides of himself, but also worked intently to soften his "hard to get along with" side. The kids and I assigned a couple of names to his alter egos. *Cooter* was the fun-loving, persistent mechanic; *Doug* was the take-charge, let's-get-our-work done, mulish guy. A couple of months before the accident, one of David's coworkers let it slip in conversation that the media team at the Saturn plant had added a few more names to David's multiple personalities. There was *Emmett*, the anal-retentive, ornery idealist; and then there was *Emmett–Damn-it*, when David would spiral into his tough, unbending, unreasonable, perfectionistic side. After his service many television coworkers, from on-air personalities to producers, directors, and editors, all told me, "That is so true about David's multiple personalities! He was a great man, but when you hired him for TV, Emmett, or Emmett–Damn-It—that was the guy you wanted on the job!" I smiled. It was so true. That nature of excellence was such a part of David's character. It didn't bother me to talk about the harder sides of this wonderfully complex man. After all, don't most of us have tucked away, hidden in the crevices, even looking attractive to others, rough, even dark sides of our nature that Christ is busy redeeming? I think it's called, for believers, sanctification, and we journey with it until our bodies give out.

* * * * * * *

Saturday came, just two days after the Rainy Day, and life was still blurry. I do remember several of David's television friends coming over to visit and asking for pictures so they could edit a music video of David's life for the service. Can you believe it? I was really happy and thankful. I remembered that drive home from the hospital when I lamented to myself that David wouldn't have a video at his service. It had really bothered me, but his wonderful friends, Danny and Terry, took the lead and saw to it that David had an amazing video, not only for the memorial service, but also for the kids, his family, and me to view forever, whenever we wanted. What a beautiful example of the faithfulness of God in the seemingly small moments of life.

EIGHT

VISITATION AND HONORING DAVID

The morning of the visitation we had the most beautiful surprise breakfast. Dear family friends, the Stringfellows, came around 7:30 a.m. and cooked breakfast for us. We enjoyed the company and the delicious waffles, bacon, and fruit. This seems like such a simple gesture, but to have wonderful fellowship and not have to worry about nourishing yourself for the long day ahead is priceless. We were now four days from the Rainy Day.

I knew the next few hours would be difficult, and if I were to get through without folding, I'd need extra prayer and support. Who better to pray with me than someone who had waded through the overwhelming waters of grief and was emerging successfully on the other side? I didn't know any widows, but I did remember my sweet friend Kimberly, who had said "good-bye for now" to her precious two-year-old daughter, Allie. No one could forget the raw courage Kimberly displayed at Allie's memorial service. It was powerful to those of us watching, and I knew I needed that anointing to help me get through the visitation and memorial service. Kimberly was available and came to the house for a private prayer time. I don't remember much about it except that it both encouraged and comforted me. She asked me to stand and hold out my hands with the palm sides up. Kimberly prayed a beautiful prayer over me while anointing my hands, feet, and forehead with oil. I felt commissioned for duty: proclaiming the Lord's goodness and faithfulness in an overwhelmingly hard circumstance of life.

While David's mom, my mom, and sister came on Thursday and Friday, we still had David's dad and sister, brother-in-law, and nephews coming from Tulsa to Nashville. David's parents had divorced twenty years earlier, and while David didn't see much of his dad, they had, in the last few years of David's life, started an email relationship. While it wasn't perfect, and David would've preferred seeing him once in a while, he took what his dad could give and was grateful.

Here's an aside: if you have relationships that aren't what you'd like them to be, consider asking God if there's something you need to do or say to make it better. It may be from no fault of your own, and it may be something years in the making. Perhaps you've already done everything you know to do. I'm mostly appealing to relationships in which you have unfinished business. Is there something you know you could do to make a situation better? Maybe it hurts too badly and you're holding out. God simply asks us for obedience. Ask Him if there's anything you're holding back, something He'd like you to move on from. He'll nudge you; trust Him. Make a phone call, write a letter, repent for bad behavior, and ask forgiveness. God is good; we can trust Him that He loves us very much.

While some of David's relationships weren't what he wanted them to be, he had made peace with these folks years earlier and did what he needed to do to make them better. That's all I'm saying: live your life so that if anything tragic comes your way, you will have no regrets. I can testify that living my life with no regrets has surely made our horrific loss a little more tolerable.

The rest of our family arrived just as visitation was starting. My friends had set up a beautiful walk down memory lane of David's life. Pictures, news articles, and awards received for his television work lined the path where friends would gather to say a few kind words to me, our kids, and the rest of the family. This memory lane walk was a great idea because it gave folks something to read, look at, and reflect on while they waited. I never dreamed that so many people would come to give their condolences. I guess it's really something you never think about—not until you're living it.

It was a really hard day, and honestly, I was so turned inward, living in the deep fog of grief, just going through the motions, that I don't remember a lot about it. I do know it was extremely honoring to David and our family. I had grace, which was not my own, overshadow me throughout that visitation time. It was Holy Spirit-inspired, and for that I'm very grateful. I overheard someone say, "Julie is actually comforting everyone who came to the church to comfort her." I don't know how I did it. Actually, I take that back; I *do* know how I did it. A strength rose up inside me. A strength that was not my own. It had been lying dormant, and it came from feeding on the Word of God and living for Him for more than twenty years; that reservoir began emerging in this hour of need.

A family that had just been handed the most devastating news a family can receive was collectively shaking fists at the mocker of the universe and saying, "His grace is sufficient! In our weakness, He is strong! Do your best, enemy of our souls, because even your best will not match the grace our Beloved pours through those who are *His!*"

The visitation lasted about five hours. I was extremely tired, and the next day wasn't going to be any easier. I needed still more grace to sprinkle over me while I slept. I'm so glad others were praying for me, because I couldn't find a way to even pray for myself.

NINE

REMEMBERING DAVID

*"Hope is the power of being cheerful in circumstances
that we know to be desperate."*

— G.K. CHESTERTON

The next morning my dear friend and hairstylist Rya came over to fix my hair for the service. While this may sound a bit unusual and rather "prom-ish," it was quite natural for our family. You see, Rya was a friend to the entire family. She'd been coming to our home for the last three years, cutting, styling, coloring, and highlighting my and Aubrey's hair. It was a blessing to her and to us. Sometimes we took pictures of our hair sessions, making an event of it or at least a scrapbooking page!

Once Rya cut Aubrey's hair for Locks of Love, the organization that takes a donor's hair and makes a wig for a child with cancer. She was also the stylist for one of my training video shoots. We loved her and she loved us. I can't imagine how painful that morning must have been for her. I don't remember a thing about it except she was there, making me beautiful for the hardest day of my life . . . saying good-bye, in public, to my best friend, my lover, the father of my children, my husband, my Cooter. I remember not really obsessing about what to wear, but being mildly curious about it. "What does a 43-year-old woman wear to her husband's funeral?" I asked no one in particular. I really wasn't into—at least for myself—the traditional funeral black. I also didn't really have an expansive wardrobe to choose from. To be honest, I can't even remember what I wore. It's just as well, I guess.

It was a cloudy winter day on February 9, 2004. The drive to the church was long and painful. There had been some decisions to make, but I honestly don't remember making many of them. Aubrey seemed to think we were doing it right, and that was good enough for me. When we got to the church, the family gathered for prayer in a room off to the side of the sanctuary. Afterward, we walked into the worship center together. I don't remember much more, honestly, only that we sang two songs and then several folks talked. We decided to honor David's memory with five preselected people talking about their memories of his life.

First was Danny Petraitis. He spoke of David as a friend. Danny was a local producer who hired David many times to shoot his projects. He spoke of friendship, admiration, and David's gift of photojournalism. He recounted a story about the two of them in St. Petersburg, Russia, trying to get footage on a dark, cloudy day. Throughout the day, the Russians would ask David, "What about light? How are we going to get the pictures without light?" And David would answer: "God's light . . . God will provide the light we need." When the time came and the shot was unfolding, at the exact time, the clouds parted and the sun peeked through in an abundance of beautiful light. Danny enthusiastically described David's unshakable faith and dependence on God. It was moving and spot-on. I'm so appreciative of Danny telling of David's life as his friend. Danny was so good to check in on the kids and me the months and years after David's relocation to Heaven. I told him many times how much I appreciated him, both his friendship to David, and later, to me. And you know what? Danny and David are together again now. Danny relocated to Heaven four years after David. A brain tumor took his earthly life, and I'm confident David was on the heavenly welcome home committee for Danny. No telling what fun they're having now. Some days, I'm jealous of them.

David's mother, Dorothy, spoke next, sharing about David as a son. Can you imagine, a mother having the courage and strength to do this? Her deep faith in God and love for her son gave her that strength. She recalled a funny story of the little boy who, under protest, hid from her in a fabric store! His hiding place was betrayed by his giggles as he watched her walk the aisles calling his name. I have such respect for Dorothy. Her heart was broken. Her precious baby boy was gone. Her pain was more than I could imagine. All I could do was pray for both of us and ask God to someday give us relief from all the horrible pain.

Aubrey and Cameron spoke next, sharing about David as a father. I can't even describe how proud I am of these two. I didn't imagine in a million years they'd want to speak. I mean, what somewhat-shy 21-year-old girl and 14-year-old boy do you know who would *ask* to speak at their daddy's memorial service? They were poignant, articulate, funny, and genuine. They both declared that God is good all the time, and all the time, God is good. Having both of them speak was appropriate. Friends appreciated David even more after hearing his children deliver an amazing and most honoring tribute to him.

I spoke last, sharing of David as my husband, soul mate,

lover, and friend. Strength rose in me that I couldn't have mustered on my own. All I could think of was: *David, my precious David. This is for you, to bring you honor. I want everyone to know how awesome you are. Weeping will come another day—actually, probably every day for a while—but not today. Today we laugh, we cheer, and we encourage one another with the awe-inspiring memory of David Hunt.*

And that's what we did. It was everything I would've wanted if I'd had weeks or months to plan it. We did it our way. The service was almost two hours and I won't apologize for that. I'm sure some were late for other obligations like work or meetings, and some had to leave the service early, but that's OK. I didn't mind. In fact, I didn't even notice.

* * * * * * *

The affirmation for my hurting heart came a week later when a kind gentleman from David's work stopped me at the Saturn Corporation Welcome Center. I had gone to Saturn to clean out David's desk, and while waiting to get my visitor's name badge, a man approached.

"Excuse me, ma'am. Are you Julie Hunt, David Hunt's widow?"

"Yes, I am."

"I was at your husband's funeral, and, well, I don't really know how to say this, but I knew your husband. He was a fine man. And, well, ma'am, that was the best funeral I've ever been to."

"Thank you, sir," I said. "I so appreciate you saying so. It's an honor. Thank you for coming, and thank you for being David's friend."

I felt accomplished in such an odd way. But it's exactly what the kids and I wanted. When I told them about the exchange I'd had with this man, Cameron spoke up and said, "Well,

Mom, I guess we put the 'fun' back in funeral, didn't we?" I laughed out loud, as did Aubrey.

"Yes, Son, I guess we did." It was so good to laugh again. We really needed that moment. My kids were so good to help me laugh once more. To this day, they never cease to amaze me.

The service may have been over, but the casseroles continued and continued. What a blessing! Generous friends brought meals for months. Some might've thought that to be an awkward intrusion, but not me! I loved not having to cook most nights. For me, it was both comforting and soothing.

TEN

GOD'S PROVISION FOR ME: AMAZING FAMILY AND FRIENDS

Some of my family stayed for several days, while others went back home the day after the service. I know it was hard for them to leave the kids and me. "Single mom" was never a thought anyone would have entertained about me.

My mom stayed for about a month. We're very close, and frankly, I needed her. My sister and I talked often on the phone. We are close sisters as well as good friends. She is one of my biggest cheerleaders in life. Her words often speak deeply to my heart. My big brother has been my champion my whole life. He is an amazing man of God, and he checked in with me weekly, offering love, guidance, and male conversation. My sister-in-law Jone was my prayer warrior. She prayed without fail for the kids and me.

David's sister Mary and her husband Mark were so very helpful to me, especially during the days immediately following the service. They were loving, patient, and respectful of my feelings. Mark is a smart businessman, and I trusted him completely. He wrote meticulous notes on a yellow legal pad left for me to read over the next few weeks. I referred to these notes several times a day. It became my business bible. It explained in detail what steps to take in the next week, two weeks, month, and year. Notes like:

The car insurance agent is _____. He will call you in the next week to give you direction about David's car and the settlement for the other driver. You are to . . .

You will need to order several death certificates. Get plenty; you'll need them. I suggest 15-20. Some places will take copies and other places will only accept an original. They are only _____ apiece. Get plenty now so you won't have to worry about it later. Your peace of mind now is very important.

David's work will be contacting you about his benefits. The lady who handles this information is _____. The man who handles it on the insurance company end is _____.

Notice the detail? This was priceless. To provide this kind of help to people in great grief is priceless; I recommend those on the "outside" looking in find ways like this to help. I was functioning at a basic level, and to some folks, looking quite well, but my brain was mush and I often comprehended little in conversation. However, I could still read, and I read through these notes word by word, many times a day, trying to understand the enormity of my new reality. I had heard the phrase "reality stinks" many times, and now I was living my own nightmare reality.

And then there was this reality to deal with . . . Mark and Mary also knew I'd need to go to the tow lot and sign a release for David's car to be crushed. They offered to go with me, and I quickly took them up on that offer. I asked the kids if they wanted to go and, much to my surprise, they did. I imagine we all were just trying to make sense of the whole tragic ordeal. To see the car, David's car, somehow helped us connect the dots of that terrible Rainy Day. I'll spare you the details of what it looked like. The older model Mercedes-Benz didn't have air bags, and we'll never know if those would have made a difference. David crossed the interstate median and was T-boned by an oncoming car. That kind of impact is hard to survive no matter the make or model of car you are driving.

The kids asked to scavenge pieces of David's car. Aubrey wanted the 300D metal emblem; Cameron asked to take the hood star emblem and several other things. I encouraged them to take whatever they wanted. As we circled the car, looking, talking, and processing, we noticed another wrecked car not far away. It was the car that crashed into David's. My stomach hurt as I mentally compared her head-on impact to David's side impact. The nose of her car, a newer model with air bags deployed, was slightly crumpled in front. The side of David's car had been pushed to the middle of the vehicle, and the frame was badly bent. The top of the car was totally ripped off, but that was done by the Jaws of Life machine used to extricate David from the wreck.

* * * * * * *

The ride home was deafeningly quiet. The reality was brutally raw. I didn't know whether to scream, sob, or just close my eyes and wish I could disappear.

Someone asked about injuries to the other driver. All we'd heard was that she'd been taken to the hospital with non-critical injuries. We returned to silence. It was then that Cameron spoke up: "Daddy's in Heaven, dancing on streets of gold! That's a good thing!" My broken boy, pulling hope from such deep places.

The grace that every one of us was experiencing was unbelievable. We couldn't stay focused on the cruelty of David's death. We had to lift our gaze and perspective upward, to life, faith, and to proclaim once again: God is good all the time. It was so beautiful how each of the kids and I supported one another during this time. When one was down, two were up. Then one would fall, but the others would rise.

We truly walked this first leg of our journey together, one moment at a time.

ELEVEN

THE PLACES ONLY SPECIAL FRIENDS CAN REACH

My friends were unbelievably available to me and for me. Tammy showed up one afternoon, a week or so after the accident, and gave me a stuffed monkey! She wanted to give me something I could cuddle. It was a perfect gift, and I snuggled Mr. Brown Monkey every night. What a heartfelt gift. Tammy is one of my friends in Heaven now. Before she left, I told her to tell my sweetie pie hello and that I'm doing fine. Actually, I asked her to tell David that we're all doing fine.

My friend Kim brought me soft yellow bunny slippers. I loved these slippers so much and almost wore them out! These are the slippers I *almost* wore to the grocery store on several occasions.

My friends came to visit as often as they could. Pam came to clean for me. We'd met at church five years earlier, and when she needed extra income, she'd clean my condo for me. We became fast friends. I was honored to read Scripture in her wedding, and when she decided to have more children, I was the first friend she told. I was also the one who was walking closely with her through her stage four cancer diagnosis. It had been a tough couple of years, but Pam was strong and determined to receive healing, beat cancer, and live to be a wife to her dear husband and mother to her five children. She was such a dear encourager to me, her grieving friend. As Anne of Green Gables would say, we were bosom friends. Pam was a wonderful friend to turn to to process some of my most painful moments that first month. Her big blue eyes would well up with tears as she would shake her head and say, "Julie, it was supposed to be me. I was to be the one who'd leave you, not David. I can't stand for you to go through all this pain. You've been the one here for me, processing this death sentence over me. I just can't believe David went before me. It wasn't supposed to have happened this way!"

These were some very huge life concepts for a 43-year-old and 37-year-old to process. We encouraged one another to cling to the only One we both knew could sort out the mess: our great big wonderful Father!

Mollie and Janet were two more dear friends who came and helped me with whatever I needed. Mollie came every Thursday for an entire year! Sometimes she helped me finish a project or clean out a drawer. Sometimes I just needed her to sit with me and listen. These two friends were both tender, kind, and so willing to be the hands and feet of Jesus for me.

My best friend since second grade, Melissa, and her husband Bill drove ten hours from Oklahoma to attend the memorial service. This was such an expression of devotion and love. I was speechless and so very grateful, even if only to hug her neck and talk for less than thirty minutes! She promised to come back in the spring to spend more time with me, and she made good on that promise in late April. We laughed, cried, remembered, ached. It was just the medicine my soul needed for comfort and nourishment.

So it's easy to see why I cherish the friendships God has been so gracious to provide for me. So many expressions of kindness and love were lavished on the kids and me during our season of heartbreak. Each and every kindness was used by the Father Himself to wrap us tightly and express His closeness to our hearts. It's just so very tender, and so precious!

TWELVE

THE TENDERNESS OF GOD: VALENTINE'S DAY 2004

"God is near to the brokenhearted and saves those who are crushed in spirit."

— PSALM 34:18

It's been nine days since the Rainy Day. This morning is like most: wake up, lay in bed a minute, get the sleepies out of my eyes, then move around in the bed, my arm flopping to the empty space beside me. Before my feet even hit the floor I remember: *Oh no, I'm a widow. What do I do now?*

Since I don't have an answer, I head downstairs for coffee and a quiet time. I don't do much reading these days. I do like a little devotional book on loss that a friend has given me. I pat myself on the back for the small accomplishments I make each day. Wake up, get out of bed, make coffee. (In the new coffee-pot!) As I think about it, that's really a huge accomplishment, because I never got a lesson from David on how to work the new coffeepot. My learning curve included a few hit-and-miss attempts, which included several pots of clear, hot water! But I have figured it out, and now I'm a coffee-making queen!

I nestle into the couch, drape an afghan over me for warmth, and try to enjoy my freshly brewed coffee. I read my Bible a bit, but put it aside quickly. It's so hard to focus on the words. I read, my mind drifts, and before I know it, I've turned three pages and can't remember one thing I've read. It would be so frustrating if I cared, but I don't. Life just seems to meld into one mind-numbing day after the other. I'm somewhat restless. I can tell it's going to be one of those mornings I dread. So, pretending to be somewhat useful, I decide to clean out a catchall basket that resides in my kitchen. You know the kind: filled with rubber bands, bobby pins, a grocery store receipt, coupons, salt packs from Sonic Drive-In, bread twist ties, and the occasional fluff of lint.

It's then that I see it. At the bottom of the basket is a red envelope, and it catches my attention. I don't recognize it, so I pick it up, open it, and can't believe my eyes.

The front of the card:

Happy Valentine's Day to My Wife

And inside, after Hallmark's beautifully written verse about love and marriage,

David wrote these words:

"I'll love you forever. You're the best thing that ever happened to me! Love, David."

This was my Valentine's Day card from the previous year, 2003. How it made it to the bottom of this basket I'll never know. But there it was, tucked in like a toddler with a teddy bear, just resting until *this* day, the day when someone greater than me orchestrated it to be read again. I was directed to that basket on this Valentine's Day morning by a tender act of kindness from a loving God. I opened that card February 14, 2003 for the first time. I open it a second time, exactly one year later, February 14, 2004, five days after I said my final good-bye to the one who picked it out and signed it a year earlier. And it is then that I realize: *God is near, and His tangible presence is with me.* He knows my heart will be so very sad on this particular day, so soon after my loss. I know He directed a specific and loving action, one that made me feel so loved and protected. The Bible says God is the widow's husband.

> *For your Maker is your husband—*
> *the Lord Almighty is His name.*
>
> ISAIAH 54:4, 5

* * * * * * *

As you can imagine, this made the rest of my day so much better. While I was sad and grieving terribly, I knew God was with me. I felt Him directing my journey and teaching me how to experience love directly from Him. Even though learning this new dance step felt terribly awkward in some moments, it also felt unusually comforting and sweet. I never would have chosen this, but somehow, *it* chose *me.*

My journey contained many more dance steps I would need to learn, but my heavenly Father is not only a good teacher, He is a most tender dance partner.

THIRTEEN

THE TERRIBLE JOURNEY OF HORRIBLE SADNESS

Nobody likes to talk about the hard stuff, much less walk through the excruciating, painful moments of life. I'm no different. But honestly, I had no map for the world in which I found myself living. I mean, one morning I woke up in my normal life, and by 3:30 that afternoon it felt like I'd switched planets. You might find yourself in this same place, or perhaps someone you love is there.

In my new planet I felt off-balance, confused, despondent, lonely, and afraid. I didn't recognize anything about life there, and I hadn't a clue as to what was expected of me. The biggest problem is that I'm a hard-core realist. I mean, black is black and white is white, real is real, and fake makes me want to throw up. But when your reality is so painful and full of trauma, it doesn't matter how real you are, it's still a crazy, incomprehensible existence.

I tried to face my grief straight up, straight on, and for real.

I wanted to punch it in the nose every morning. If I hurt, I hurt. If it was a bad morning, I said, "It's a bad morning." If I felt peaceful, I'd say, "I'm OK." I really didn't know what else to do but look at each day for what it was: a terrible journey through a horrible sadness. I don't think I could've covered my pain if I'd even wanted to. It was much too difficult just to put on a happy face and muster through. Some days, I couldn't even try to help others feel better about being around me. I was a sad, mixed-up mess, for sure.

But you know what? I decided I just couldn't wear a mask through the circumstances I'd landed in. I wasn't afraid of the messiness that was now called my life—I just had to live through it. And I'm sorry if others couldn't deal with the transparent way I had to live through my pain.

God hadn't removed me from the pain, and yet I knew for a fact that He was with me every moment of every day in that pain. I treated His presence as though He was really with me, like a person who lived with me. This realist didn't hold back; after all, He's supposed to be my husband now, right? So I let Him be just that—as much as I knew how. I spoke out loud to Him—a lot. "You're still here, right? You haven't left like David did, right?" I never heard an answer back from Him, but I knew I wasn't alone just the same. He walked and napped with me, He held and comforted me, and He carried me through the entire terrible journey of horrible sadness when I let Him.

I knew God was a good God, and if He'd allowed this horrible accident, then there had to be some really good treasures just on the other side. But my reality was still the same. No matter how solid I was in my faith, no matter how great our support system was, Aubrey, Cameron, and I had a deep loss that had to be worked through.

MY JOURNAL ENTRY FROM FEBRUARY 24, 2004

I'm 20 days past the accident. Everyone has been nice, encouraging, and so very helpful. I've received many phone calls from friends both in town and out of town. My family checks on me many times a day, and the meals for Cameron and me just keep coming. Lots of kind folks offer to help me do just about anything that needs to be done. It's both comforting and practical. I mean, Cameron needs a ride home from soccer practice, and I'll think I can do it that morning . . . but by afternoon, I just can't function. Unfortunately, grief has a direct link to unpredictable, impractical, and unexplainable emotions. One minute I'm fine and strong, and the next minute I'm a puddle of memories and extremely broken. My pain is almost unbearable and my sadness swallows me alive. I turn to the left, and pain meets me. I run to the right, and it's still there. What's even more perplexing is the fact that in the midst of such deep despair, a flicker of hope flashes across my mind. I'm going to be all right. I know I'm going to be all right. The kids will be all right and we'll make it, eventually, on down the road. It's just today. I'm so unsure about today, right now. Will I make it right now, this moment in time? The loss feels so very deep, indescribably deep.

I must be in the shock and disbelief stage of grief. I just can't believe it's over. My time on earth with David is over . . . it's just gone. I have my memories, but are they enough to last my lifetime? All I know is I want him here with me, now. I'm not ready to say good-bye. I just wasn't ready to say good-bye.

MY JOURNAL, FEBRUARY 28, 2004

The shock and disbelief still haunt me. I want to get to David and tell him what's happening to me. I have such an overpowering need to say to him, "Look what you did! You died in the middle of our dreams!" While this sounds angry, I don't think I'm really angry. I just want to talk to him about what's happened the last few weeks because we used to talk about everything! I feel like the most important event that I've ever been through has just happened and I can't talk with or even get to the person I need to discuss it with the most! I'm sad, frustrated, and yeah, maybe just a little bit angry too.

JOURNAL, FEBRUARY 29, 2004

I've missed three Sundays of church. I've got to go back, but I have very mixed feelings about it. I'm anxious about returning. Not necessarily to see the people, but just going back to the building where I said good-bye to David. Maybe this is a great case for having a memorial service at a funeral home rather than your family church. Hmm . . . that would've been good information to know before now! Oh well, I guess I'm ready to go back next Sunday . . . yes, that seems like a good plan.

FOURTEEN

My Unknown Future

"Don't be afraid to trust an unknown
future to a known God."

—Corrie ten Boom

My English II professor, freshman year in college, allowed students to choose a focus of study. I chose the subject of Death and Dying, a rather worrisome choice for sure. You might wonder why a beautiful, bright young girl would choose such a morbid topic for her section of English. I'm kind of wondering that myself, and while I knew it was an odd choice, the fact of the matter was I was interested in the death process and the afterlife. I was still formulating my faith and belief system and, unfortunately, my life experiences to that point had made me well acquainted with death. By my freshman year in college I had experienced the loss of two grandparents and a boyfriend.

In fifth grade I witnessed my grandfather die in my father's arms. In ninth grade my grandmother died in her sleep. It was rather shocking and hit my mother hard. Two weeks later, the love of my young life died tragically in a car accident, just three days before beginning his senior year of high school. So here it was my sophomore year, and I was already "the widow" of my small high school. I had no one to talk with and no one to walk me through those rough teen years, let alone someone to help my with my aching, broken heart. No wonder by the time I got to college I was interested in what the heck happens to us when we die!

I had so many questions and so little knowledge and understanding. Little did I know within the next five years I would experience three more sudden and tragic deaths: another grandfather; my dad, at only 55 years old (plus, I was pregnant with my first child when he died); and my best friend, who was kidnapped, raped, and brutally murdered. It almost seems too much, doesn't it? One young girl, twenty-four years old, experiencing so much loss at such a young age.

Still, I am confident that growing up in a Christian home, while far from perfect, gave me a strong foundation of support when the circumstances of life crashed in. The Bible, and several devotional books, kept me grounded and steady when the waves of unrelenting grief seemed overwhelming. I believed the Bible and trusted that God was going to heal my broken heart and deliver me, whether I understood Him or not. His Word comforted me.

"Because he loves me," says the Lord, "I will rescue him. I will protect him, for he acknowledges My name. He will call upon me, and I will answer him; I will be with him in trouble, I will deliver him and honor him. With long life will I satisfy him and show him my salvation."

PSALM 91:14-16

I would pray these words over myself, asking God to rescue me and show me his unfailing kindness. I asked Him to wrap His mighty arms around me and show me His sincere, unwavering, and unconditional love. I knew as I cried out to God that He would hear me. I knew He was close by with tender compassion. I asked Him to let me feel Him right beside me, to recognize Him as my head, my shepherd, my husband.

In my complete and utter brokenness, I experienced God like I'd never experienced Him before. I had known Him in the highlights of my life, like winning a piano competition or a spot on the baton twirling team. But in this valley, where I needed Him like never before, I was receiving an expression of His deep, abiding love that caused me to fall deeper in love with Him. I wasn't out of the woods of grief by a long shot, but I felt He was giving me a deposit of beautiful things to come. If I could just hang on and trust Him, He would turn all my heartache into something beautiful. Jars of Clay, a popular Christian band, did the song "Something Beautiful." It ministered deeply to my aching heart. One of the lines says, "Change this something normal into something beautiful"[2]—and that was my prayer.

I tried to come to grips with my heartache. I cried almost all day, every day. I never questioned God, but I questioned *myself*, all the time. Was I strong enough to hang on? Would I let Him wrap His arms of love around me, around all of this mess, and let Him change it into something beautiful? I needed help, a lot more help than I was getting. The practical help given by amazing friends was wonderful and did provide relief from burdens too big to handle by myself. But still, the horrible weight of what had happened to us all felt, at times, crushing. I knew I was on an extremely long road to wholeness. I knew nothing else to do but get out of bed, eat, try to parent my children as best as I could, and trust that God was bigger than the mountain of grief before me.

In my deepest wound, I saw Your Glory, and it dazzled me.

St. Augustine

JOURNAL ENTRY, MARCH 6, 2004

Grief is a curious invader. It leaves for several hours at a time, then, in one moment, a memory washes over, stirs up loss, and leaves a heavy weight of grief behind. I gasp to stay above the waterline, for if it overtakes me, I may never come up. Bobbing, just at the surface and lost in the treacherous waters of doubt and despair. On these waves of uncertainty and pain, I know I am not alone. Jesus surfs them with me, even holding my head upright when the fierce waters threaten to bury me forever.

This is one of those unbearable mornings where my grief is choking me. I can literally feel its grip tightening around my throat, cutting off my air passage at a hideously slow rate. I throw my head back, trying to loosen its death grip on me, but to no avail. I bite my lip and writhe in pain. I scream out, "Can a body survive such excruciating emotional pain? Will I make it until noon—or even 10 a.m.?"

I didn't know what to do except feel it. Let the pain wash over me in a flood of sorrow. Let it beat me and pummel me over and over again. I wanted to scream, groan, wail, and cry. My face would be soaking wet with tears and my nose would be annoyingly stopped up at the same time! I would get up just to wash my face and blow my nose. I would pause at the doorway. I'd moan in deep guttural tones. I hit my head against the door frame, and then I was raising my voice, even yelling.

"What am I going to do now? I can't go on. I can't. *I can't do this!*"

I would hit my head over and over. I didn't care about bruising, cuts, blood, or even brain damage. It's my heart damage

I'm worried about! My heart is broken, half of it ripped from my chest weeks ago. Everything I knew—my husband, friend, lover, and father of my kids . . . my provider, protector, defender, and strength—*everything is gone!* I can't go on without him. I don't want to go on without him. *God, this can't be real. This can't be your plan!* My heart aches; I've never felt such loss, such hopelessness, such despair. I take a few more steps into the bathroom. I look in the mirror and pause. My reflection is death: death of dreams, death of vision, death of hope, death of life. "Poor Julie!" I sigh aloud. "Girl, how are you going to get out of this one? How do you ever get past this?" Yes, I am talking out loud to myself.

My crying continues for most of the day. It's just so very, very hard. I pull myself together after an hour or so. I'm exhausted, overwhelmed, unmotivated, and pretty much a mess. I cuddle Gretta and ask her what we're going to do. Like I think she'll actually answer me! What's wrong with me? Am I losing it? I'm talking to a dog! We sit for most of the day. The only time I'm outside is to take her for a walk. We don't go far. I'm like a scared little mouse, fearfully scurrying out of my hole, though only for a few steps, and then scampering quickly back inside.

Since I don't know much of anything about anything anymore, I'm not anxious to get out and live. I just don't have a lot of interest in the outside world at the moment. One thing I do know is Cameron will be home from school soon and I've got to get my act together before then. I need to stop crying by 2:30 p.m. so my face will be less puffy, my nose not as red, and my eyes not as swollen. When he asks me, "How's it going, Mom?" I can answer him honestly: "Right now, I'm good. Better. 'Cause you're home." I pray to God my 14-year-old never asks me, "So, Mom, how were you at noon today?" Or, "How will you be doing tonight, when I'm doing my homework?"

I tell him that I'm just upstairs reading or taking a hot bath. But the truth? Seriously, my honest answers would be these:

Son, I am so lonely I want to just scream!

My bed is so big and so cold without Daddy in it that I'm overwhelmed and afraid to sleep in it by myself.

I'm afraid that I won't make it, and then you'll be an orphan!

. . . But, of course, I can't actually say these things to Cameron.

You want more truth? How about this: Mommy's not doing so well these days. I'm going through this hell called loss, going through it the best I can. I'm just a little new to these dance steps. I don't quite have all the moves yet.

But I'll get there. I'll be fine.

. . . And my prayer these days?

God, please hold me. Comfort me, love me, and please, God, help me not to do anything stupid today. Amen.

FIFTEEN

Facing Up to the Firsts

A smooth sea never made a skillful sailor.

—Unknown

The first big event after David's accident was Valentine's Day, and I've already described the beautiful way God took such special care of me.

But there were plenty of other "firsts." Each had its own distinct bittersweet nature.

BIRTHDAY NUMBER 44

My 44th birthday came next. When I was asked what I wanted to do, it actually felt good to say, "Let's party!" The five weeks had been so full of sadness that I wanted to try a reverse strategy, and it worked, even if just for a day. My friends were so incredible: probably twenty-five or more came with food, gifts, and laughter. It really felt good to visit with others and find out what was going on in their lives. I felt loved and honored. I really do have special friends. I cherish every one of them and what they've each brought to my life. If you know someone going through this type of pain, please see that you're a great friend to that person, and make sure others surround them with love as well.

EASTER 2004

Easter was really the first major holiday after the accident, and I was not looking forward to it. I love my Lord and Savior Jesus Christ, but honestly, my heart didn't feel much like celebrating His death, burial, and resurrection. It was a hard holiday for me, and I just didn't want to put a lot into it. I'm sure our dear friends from out of town, Jamie and Larry Williams, sensed this sadness as well. They called and invited themselves to Nashville to spend the Easter holiday with Aubrey, Cameron, and me. I was so very glad they did. I never would have had the foresight to think about this holiday and what it would look like, alone, without David. I don't remember much about the weekend, but I was glad that Aubrey, Cameron, and I had our dear friends to lean on for moral support.

As I look back, the only other thing I wrote about Easter in my journal was that I should not have gone Easter dress shopping by myself!

JOURNAL ENTRY, AROUND EASTER, 2004

I don't think grieving women should go shopping alone and decide for themselves what looks good on their body. I guess I should give three cheers for myself that I felt mentally strong enough to get dressed, leave the house, and drive to a store. But the unfortunate news is I picked out a calamine lotion pink dress with jacket. Are you gagging yet? Well, let me tell you more. The jacket was pink and black stripes, and those stripes were five inches wide and horizontal, not vertical. And my body? With all the delicious comfort food delivered to my house on a semi-daily basis, I had put on at least 10 pounds in two and a half months.

I also might mention that I have "the grief look," draped across my face. There is definitely a heaviness you can see on a grieving person's face. I recognize it on others and I see it on my own face. Nothing can erase brokenness that is reflected from the eyes.

Thankfully, I was too deep in my grief to have known or noticed this in "real time," and my friends were much too dear to say a word. They just loved my children and me and helped us through the first holiday without David. I'm very grateful for good friends like the Williamses.

Other firsts throughout the year came and went: Father's Day, David's birthday, the kids' birthdays, Thanksgiving, Christmas. I dreaded these events, even grew somewhat anxious about them coming, but it did no good. The "firsts" after any trauma will have as much power over you as you chose to give them.

I realized I could work myself into an emotional frenzy or I could tell God, "I'm hurting and I need more grace." He would fill my cup to overflowing and I would get through the firsts, each and every one. I'd wake up the next morning and even feel a bit victorious that death had not been the winner. Life is the winner, and I was choosing to live each and every morning. I remember saying, "David may be gone, living somewhere else right now, but I'm still here. I'm still alive, here on earth, and I must live here until He (God) says to live with Him in Heaven!"

JOURNAL, MARCH 15, 2004

My spiritual life is gasping for air. I have no idea where we are going in the turn we made on Feb. 5th. It all has me so shocked and surprised that all I can do is sit and rest while my curiosity grows. God, what are you doing with my life? I trust you completely, but what are you doing? I'm barely 44 years old and I'm a widow? Unbelievable!

The kids and I watched a Lord of the Rings movie Sunday after church. A scene in the movie haunts me. I'm still chewing on it and wondering how to apply it to my situation. When Frodo questions the mission to take the ring to Mordor, he tells Gandalf:

"I wish the ring had never come to me. I wish none of this had ever happened."

Gandalf replies: "So do all who live to see such times, but that is not for them to decide. All you have to decide is what to do with the time that is given to you."[3]

With that conversation, young Frodo finds the strength and courage to move on with the task assigned to him, to get the ring to the fires of Mordor. He understands his mission, and it doesn't matter how dark or dangerous the task is or how fearful he is of doing it. What matters is that he is chosen; this little pure-in-heart hobbit has been chosen to cast the ring into the fires of Mordor and overcome evil!

Everyone who has been hit with the hard pain that life can bring—whether it's trauma, suffering, or loss—each person has a decision to make. *What will I do with the time that is given to me?* Really, that's the question.

What will *I* do with the time given to me?

Could it be that what happened to David is now part of the plan, not a diversion from it? I have a decision to make: to trust God so completely that even in deep sorrow it can be well with my soul. Oh, such a thought! Or, I can choose not to. But how can all of this ever be well with my soul? God. God is the answer to that question. God can do all things. He is able to make all things well with my soul. Isn't He full of mighty thoughts, deeds, and higher ways?

I don't expect to know and understand what He's doing. I can't discern His every plan. I'm not supposed to! He's God; I'm not! Do I know it all myself? No! For if I know it all, then I might not need Him! And I do need Him. Desperately.

I'm OK, even fine, with not understanding right now. And I do believe, in time, as I press into Him and get to know His ways better, that I may someday have understanding. And that's OK with me.

SIXTEEN

WHEN GRIEF
MEETS REALITY

I have a delightful friend I've spiritually mentored for more than eighteen years. She is precious to me and I love her to pieces. She was so good to call me, almost daily after the accident, and ask, "Need anything? I'm heading out." Or, "Just checking in. How's the day going?" I appreciate her love and support so very much, even today. I know this friend is a "lifer," one who will be there for me no matter what.

A couple of months after the accident, during one of her check-in times, I found out she was really struggling with David's relocation to Heaven. We talked a bit when suddenly she blurted out, "Julie, I'm really struggling with this. I don't understand why David died. I mean, ya'll are the perfect family. You've done everything right! You and David loved each other, you have fantastic kids, you love God, and you go to church every Sunday and help so many people in so many ways. Why in the world would God let this happen?"

I took a deep breath, gathered my thoughts quickly, and readied myself to give an answer according to my faith. My mind was racing on so many levels. On one level, I felt affirmed, complimented. We were an awesome family. We had made many best and right decisions for twenty-two years. All four of us—two parents and two kids—had lived strong love, tough love, pure love, and unconditional love. But on the other hand, I felt like saying, "The greater question is: Why not David? Do any of us have a get-out-of-jail-free card?

And then, if I'm totally honest, on another level, I agreed with her. *What the heck, God? Why us, why David, why me?* I didn't like this level, and when I found myself sinking to this place, I did everything I could to exit quickly. But in my gnawing pain, every once in a while, I would turn inward and have a pity party. I knew better than to attend a party like this. The primary goal of a pity party is to suck the party-giver into a black hole that's extremely difficult to escape.

Again, I gathered my thoughts and said to my friend: "I know it seems unfair. David was one of the good ones, wasn't he? But my friend, let me share with you what God told me when I asked Him this very question last week."

I told her I had been wrestling hard with grief and the Father held me, listening intently to my struggling heart. After about fifteen minutes of weeping, questioning, and begging Him for answers, demanding that He show me His justice in all of this, He broke through my outburst and asked *me* a few questions.

"Julie, who would *you* have picked to die in that car wreck? A homeless man, a lazy man, a man who was cheating on his wife? A no-good rotten scoundrel?"

God was saying to me: "Who, Julie, who . . . would *you* have told *me* to pick?" I hung my grieving head in shame. What was I thinking? Who was I to make these kinds of decisions? I'm not God. I'm not the judge of the living or the dying. I'm confused, hurting, grieving, and accusing my heavenly Father of wrongdoing, missing a mark, and messing up my life. So I prayed: "I'm sorry, Father. Please forgive me."

He gently reminded me: "Julie, sweetie, David was ready to go. He'd lived a wonderful, albeit short life on earth. But he lived well and, most importantly, he'd made the exchange, to give his life to Jesus Christ and have his sin redeemed. He was born again through the shed blood of Jesus. He was ready to meet his maker."

I felt so honored. Even in my brokenness, God was meeting me and challenging me to look up and see my salvation through this journey.

God, in His mercy, had directed me to read and meditate on Job two months before David's accident. I didn't understand why at the time, but now I understand perfectly. I thought about the book of Job, chapter 1, verses 20-22. Job's words in this passage came at the news of the loss of his livestock, servants, children, and their wives. And when this happened, the Bible says, Job fell to the ground in worship.

"Naked I came from my mother's womb, and naked I will depart. The Lord gave and the Lord has taken away; may the name of the Lord be praised." In all this, Job did not sin by charging God with wrongdoing.

Job had experienced so much sudden and tragic loss, but did you catch his response? When he received the terrible news, one bad report after another, his response was praise! He worshiped God and did not sin by accusing God of wrongdoing! Oh, how I wanted to walk in that attitude of heart! My heart's desire was to wake up with praise on my lips, ready to receive the new truckload of mercy the Father had for me each and every morning! In this moment, God, an attentive, caring, and good Father, didn't leave me unprepared in my journey.

He knew that I would need Scripture like this in my mind, on my heart, and at the ready for His Holy Spirit to draw it up and out. He would comfort me and, most of all, remind me that I am not alone. I'm so very, very grateful.

* * * * * * *

I was moving along my journey and it was almost summer. I looked forward to a new season, both literally and figuratively. The sun, now shining on most days, was so wonderful, and while I was learning my new dance steps and trying to trust God daily, I still experienced great sadness and many questions. I tried not to ask why, but it was hard, in my honest dialogue with Him, not to ask, "Why did you let this happen? Why didn't you stop the accident? Why didn't you let the heroic measures by the Vanderbilt doctors work?"

These *Why?*-type questions didn't work well for me. They seemed to suck me down into a hole of despair, and they only worked to focus my thoughts on my circumstances. I never found comfort looking inward, only more despair and exasperation. When I asked the *Why?*-type questions, I never came away with answers, so I finally decided to avoid, as much as possible, asking why. It felt so childish and me-centered. You know, there's a whole big world out there, and if I truly believed that my loving, kind, compassionate Father, Creator of everything I see, allowed this turn in my journey, then I could live with and even come to terms with the fact that maybe He could turn it all around for my good, just like He promises us in His Word.

I came to ask myself some pretty hard questions. I *say* I trust God, but do I really? Did I trust Him as much as I had professed? Did I trust Him in little things, big things, in everything? What I began to realize was that my continually asking why was, in fact, like chipping away at the wall called Trusting

God. These bricks in my personal wall of faith were built from years of believing God, reading His Word, and trusting Him with my life. If I began to doubt the very place where my faith was built, could I chip away enough that the wall would start to crumble? That frightened me even more than not having tidy answers to the deepest, gnawing questions.

So I forced myself to come to this conclusion: "I trust you, Father. I don't have anywhere else to go!" I would say those words aloud, with the same resolve of Peter, who, in John 6:68, said to Jesus, "Where would we go, Lord? *You* have the words of eternal life!"

SEVENTEEN

Two Lions Come to Live with Us

I knew that many of our family and friends were struggling in their own private mourning pool, one I knew little about. It's kind of hard—and a bit unrealistic—to mourn with the spouse of the dearly departed. There's a kind of unspoken agreement that her grief trumps yours, so you should never try to compare your broken hearts. But loss is large and complicated. I knew others were hurting too. I simply didn't know how to help them, so in most cases they grieved without me.

My mom struggled with David's loss, but in addition, it was really hard for her to leave her baby girl and grandchildren in Nashville to walk through their grief alone. We talked on the phone often. She was instrumental in helping me sort through my feelings of hopelessness because she'd been widowed eleven years earlier. The morning of April 22, just two and a half months after David's death, she called and told me of a dream she'd had the night before. My mom's words stunned me.

"You know, Julie, I don't dream much, right? And if I do, I *never* remember it the next morning. But this dream is different. I remember it, and it feels like it wasn't a dream, but that it really happened." She went on to relate that she was staying with the kids and me at the condominium. And, in her dream . . . I was letting two full-grown lions live in the house with me, a male and a female. Mom said she was beside herself, anxious, afraid, thinking any move we made could make the lions attack. She marveled at how unconcerned I was that two lions lived in my home. I was matter-of-fact and even unafraid, behaving like everything was normal. She said, "I don't know why you would let these two lions live in your house! It's dangerous!" The female lion paced back and forth throughout the house, many times a day. The male lion was present but not seen as much as the female. At night, when we were getting ready for bed, I took a small child and laid her down alongside the male lion. Mom said she went berserk. "Julie! Why in the world would you lay that child by that lion? This is not right, not safe!" She said I calmly turned to her and said, "But Mom, this is where the child sleeps. She'll be fine." And that was the end of her dream.

For the next three days we pondered what this dream could mean. When my mom talked to my brother, he listened but had no interpretation. After the phone call, he told his wife Jone about the dream and, without missing a beat, Jone said, "I have the interpretation for the dream. The two lions are God's gift to Julie. The male lion is Jesus. He is in the home, lives there, and is the silent, guiding influence for Julie and the kids. He is the strong, confident presence in the home, like a husband would provide. The female lion represents the church, specifically Julie's home church, but really more than that, the body of Christ. It provides the practical, emotional, hands-on support for this family in crisis. The female lion is pacing back and forth, busy coming and going throughout the home with phone calls, meals, support, and love. The lions are providing the calm, steady flow of God's love.

"The small child is Julie, your momma's baby. It's hard for your momma to trust Julie to Jesus right now. Her mother's heart is broken, not only for the loss of a fine son-in-law, but the path her baby girl must now walk. Your mom is eight hundred miles away. She must trust God to be able to take care of Julie, even in this painful time. Julie lies down in the evening with Jesus right by her side. He is all she needs to protect, comfort, support, and strengthen her. Your mom must learn the lessons of trusting God just like Julie—actually, just like all of us!"

And that was that. A glorious dream and interpretation that gave each of us profound personal comfort. This rings so true to the God we serve. Thank you, God, for this precious gift.

JOURNAL, MAY 26, 2004

My condo neighbor is so sweet! She brought by Nichole Nordeman's newest album, Brave. Don't you just love that title? Brave! I want to be brave with all my heart! I don't want to live the rest of my life scared, timid, and afraid. I want to live the life God called me to live: bold, courageous, and fearless! I'm going to love this album, I just know it! I already love her music because my David loved her music. Her song "Legacy" is what Terry and Danny used for David's memorial video. Yes, I'll probably wear this album out soon because I want to be brave . . . Lord, make me brave again![4]

JOURNAL, JUNE 6, 2004

I want to read the Bible. I know it would be good for me to meditate on God's Word, but it's still so hard to read and get much of anything from it. I think my brain went on vacation and still hasn't returned. I try to read and still can't remember what it says. I keep trying, but some days I know it's useless. Other days, I read something like this and it keeps me stirred up, confused, and wondering if I'll ever have peace of mind again:

But whoever listens to me will live in safety and be at ease, without fear of harm *(Proverbs 1:33).*

Have you ever read this verse before? I had read it many times and then had the thought: *What great news!* It seemed as though the Bible was saying we get a pass to pull out whenever life seems unsafe. Who wouldn't want that? If I listen to God, I will be guaranteed that nothing will ever happen to me. God will keep me (and all believers) safe from harm, things like sickness, disease, trauma . . . fatal accidents . . . or any other bad thing. Oh yes, that would be great news, if only it were true!

It can certainly be problematic when we read verses out of context or even treat the Word of God like a magic lantern; we simply rub it in hopes that all kinds of good things will come out! God's Word is truth, sovereign, and meant to be read, studied, and brought alive by the Holy Spirit who lives inside all believers. But I hit the proverbial wall (pardon the pun!) when I read this verse after David's accident. I found it to be very troubling, because it made me feel like God had dropped the ball. My David didn't live in safety on that rainy morning, nor did he feel at ease; he was in fact harmed.

It made my heart sad to question God's Word, so I went to the Father and asked Him about it, actually chewing on this Scripture, and several others, day and night, trying to gain understanding and peace. As His goodness would have it, ten days later He gave me understanding, and it gave me great peace. I hope it will do the same for you.

JOURNAL, JUNE 17, 2004

[Writing to myself] Julie, do you believe the Word of God?
Do you believe what it says with all of your heart?
Both answers: Yes!

Julie, in Isaiah 49:16 it says that God has written your name on His hand. In Isaiah 41:13 it says that He takes hold of your right hand and tells you to not be afraid. Do you believe what it says, Julie?

Yes, I do believe what it says.

And then I pondered this a little more before continuing my journaling . . .

It's my focus, isn't it, Lord? Or, rather, how I'm looking at life, from my vantage point on earth, down here, right?

Yes. Keep going, Julie.

God, you are looking at this from your view, the big, huge picture. Wow. You're looking at a whole life's journey, from beginning to end. It must look so different from what I can see.

I pondered and chewed on this for most of the morning, and this is what He showed me in my dialogue with Him. . . .

So, you asked if I believe Your Word, that I'm actually in Your hand, and I told you "yes." So to keep going in that train of thought, I'm safe from harm in your hand, because when I gave my life to Jesus, my sin, my death sentence was covered, paid in full, right?

I closed my eyes and thought. It's like the word *death* is printed on my forehead. But when I came to Jesus, He erased that word on my forehead. He changed it to *LIFE*. *Life* is the banner over me, along with His love. I will live forever, and I am living forever—starting now. Eternity began for me the moment I said, "Jesus, I choose you. You are my Savior, and you are my Lord."

The real me, the spirit inside me, will never die and will live forever.

> *Oh, Father! This is why it's hard for me to say that David died! It's not because I don't want to face the reality of the accident, it's because he really didn't die! The real him, his spirit, relocated, just lives somewhere else now, Heaven, with YOU! His body died, but he didn't die!! In you, none of us die! We NEVER face death! Which is why Proverbs 1:33—"But whoever listens to me will live in safety and be at ease, without fear of harm"—doesn't hit me so hard anymore, because this Old Testament verse now has new discovery in light of what Jesus brings to us in the New Testament. We who are in Jesus will always live in safety because the evil one CANNOT touch the real us, our spirit-man! We can be at ease, without fear of harm, because our enemy has NO POWER over us because the provision of the blood of Jesus is life eternal!! HALLELUJAH!!*

I now believe that many verses I had thought about and studied "BC" (before Christ) make more sense when viewed through this revelation.

> *Precious in the sight of the LORD is the death of his faithful servants (Psalm 116:15).*

It's precious because *He* knows where we're going!

> *Where, O death, is your victory? Where, O death is your sting? (1 Corinthians 15:55)*

There is no victory in death! Jesus removed it because, when our earthly bodies experience death, they decay, but we go on to live forever with Jesus! Since death is dealt with, there's no sting either! The sting was a sinful nature. But Jesus took care of that, so . . . no sting!

That's why Paul says, in 1 Corinthians 15:57:

But thanks be to God, who gives us the victory through our Lord Jesus Christ! Therefore, my dear brothers and sisters, stand firm. Let nothing move you.

And Paul goes on to say in Philippians 1:21:

For to me, to live is Christ and to die is gain.

I was beginning to realize: Oh wow! Oh *wow*! God, this is amazing! I'm blown away at your merciful comfort to my soul!

And I went on from there, the next day, with revelation upon revelation. I felt like my brain was exploding, but in a good way!

JOURNAL, JUNE 18, 2004

You know what? David's death on earth wasn't the ultimate tragedy! The ultimate tragedy would be if Aubrey, Cameron, and I lived the rest of our lives on earth like it was! We must break through our limited, grief-covered view and see this from God's perspective. We need to climb up in His lap and see all of this from HIS view. I bet it's really, really good from up there! Hope is rising. . . . Hope is rising!!! In your face, devil! God is bigger, and He's so very good!

I'm realizing that I'm on a journey, actually an adventure, with God. I can't rush this or wish it away. It's stinks but it's beautiful all at the same time. I have learned so much. I still have so much to learn! I think God is going to just reveal it to me one moment at a time. As I can bear it. Just like a gentleman, isn't it?

JOURNAL, JUNE 18, 2004 (LATER THAT DAY)

I'm still thinking about all of this, trying to understand what God is inviting me to learn . . . think, Julie, think . . . trust, Julie, trust . . .

According to what Paul wrote in 2 Corinthians 4:8 I can be:

A		B
hard pressed	but not	crushed
perplexed	but not	in despair
persecuted	but not	abandoned
struck down	but not	destroyed

So, when evil looms in our world today, hovering over us, hissing, and even swiping a vicious claw at God's people, we can be A but not B. If we feel like B, according to the Bible, we need to run to Jesus for shelter because the enemy is turning our beliefs to something that God's Word says we don't have to tolerate!

Keep reading in 2 Corinthians 4:16-18. Don't lose heart!

Fix your eyes on what is unseen, because what we see is temporary, but what we don't see, is eternal!!!

David has slipped over to what I cannot see. Remember when I told him, just before he slipped over, "If what you see is better, go on." And that's just what he did! He squeezed my hand, in ultimate love, support, compassion, and joy and went on ahead—to occupy new territory in the kingdom. Here's a visual to what I'm thinking, Lord:

We're going along in life and BOOM! God allows X to happen. X can look bad, evil, cause sorrow, be confusing.

But to God, X can:

1 – be part of His bigger plan
2 – be worked together for good
3 – accomplish great things
4 – advance the Kingdom of God

We must always remember, we are working together for the kingdom of God and advancing that kingdom. We are given over to death for Jesus' sake, every day, so His life will be revealed in our body (2 Corinthians 4:10)!

EIGHTEEN

THE DANCE STEPS OF GRIEF: TWO STEPS FORWARD, THREE STEPS BACK

JOURNAL, JULY 6, 2004

I'm doing pretty well, but to be honest, this is a much longer journey than I imagined. I think I'm trying to race through it, get to the end, but what I'm realizing is, it's not a race, it's a journey, and no matter how hard I try to get through it, it just ain't gonna happen that way.

We got through more of the firsts, like Father's Day and the Fourth of July. It's not easy and, to tell you the truth, I think we're all feeling a bit numb. It's really hard to know what to do, how to behave. Is there something we need to be doing? What does the "Grieving Family's Handbook," say? Do we just talk about it a little more each day, as we can handle? Honestly, what's left to say? We still miss him. Yeah, it hurts. It is what it is, and some days, it sucks!

This is a day in the life of a grieving family, and it is all so very normal. We were still in the cycle of: sometimes I'm good, and sometimes I'm not. One day, one of us would hit rock bottom; the others would be OK. And then we'd switch; the one who had plummeted days earlier would crawl out, look around, and be OK, but find one of the others sinking. It was both a blessing and a terrible time, especially to walk through it with your kids. And dealing with my grief around other people was next to impossible. For instance, I'd go to church and folks would say really nice things. Like, "How are you?" And, "Can I do anything for you?" And I'd get angry on the inside and think, *Wow! I can't go anywhere and just be . . . just forget that I'm a widow with a stinky life!* And then I'd go somewhere and no one would mention what I'd been through. *No one* would acknowledge, "Well, it's true. You're a widow, with a sad, stinky life." And that would make me angry. It provoked pity, like: *Don't they know or care what I'm going through!* It was in this season of grief that I realized: No one is going to help this get better. I'm just going to have to muddle through my life somehow, but I really don't know how.

One day, I couldn't help myself. My grief was a raging, rushing river of despair. And in a navel-gazing moment (I know, I ignored my own warning signs!) my troubled, sad heart could not be silenced. In a fit of desperation I screamed at God, "Why did you let this happen!? . . . You took the wrong parent. It should've been me! I don't know how to live without David. I don't know how to do this!"

And I heard, with my heart, a voice say, "Julie, stop asking why! It doesn't help! Let me answer a different question for you. Ask me, 'How? How will I turn this tragedy around for good? How will I sustain you and the kids? How will I provide for you to not only survive, but have victory through your grief?'"

Through tears and a trembling voice, I said aloud, "OK, I give up. I surrender the why. But please show me how we'll do this."

"Let's dance, Daughter. Let me take you in my arms and love you back to life."

And for the better part of an hour, I let God treat me like a new bride on a dance floor with her daddy. He twirled me around and delighted in my every move. I laughed, I mis-stepped, I cried, I twirled, I rested. That morning changed everything. My perspective was much less inward-focused. My eyes looked up and trusted Him who is able to keep me from falling.

That was the day I realized that peace is available on *this* side of eternity. As I gave myself once again to my Creator, my Father God, my Abba-Daddy, letting Him choose and lead my troubled heart to safer waters, I felt a twinge of hope. I realized that God understood my grief. After all, didn't He grieve too when He gave His only Son, Jesus? Why do you think He had to turn His head, and Jesus felt forsaken at the cross? I said it aloud: "God, you grieve with me, don't you? But you grieve with *hope*. I want to learn how to grieve with hope too." My honest, heartfelt prayer was answered that day. I started walking my road of sorrow *with* my Daddy. With God.

Some days I missed David so deeply I couldn't function. Many days that first year found me in excruciatingly painful sorrow. My friends may have known it, but many did not. It seemed harder to let them into the pain on some days. Many days I chose to just keep them out and say I was sad but coping. Honestly, I think some of them were relieved when I chose to handle it this way. I grieved so openly and honestly in the beginning that I'm sure my life was rather sad and tiring for some. And as I got further away from the Rainy Day, I became less and less sure of what was expected of me.

Was I to behave a certain way, think a particular way? I just wasn't sure what it was supposed to look like. Grief got really tricky when we got close to one year after the accident. I longed to find yet another manual—maybe this one should be called "Handbook for the Grieving Heart–Year 2." And you know what? I think I was living and writing my own book. My cup of sorrow had to be drunk by me and only me. No one else could drink it for me or with me. As I curled up in my big, empty bed, with my snuggly, faithful, and warm Gretta-dog and my cuddle-monkey from Tammy, I pulled out my journal.

I am grieving with hope and rejoicing in suffering. God fills me every day with exactly what I need for that day. I trust Him; He's promised to complete the good work He's begun in me. As John Henry Newman said, and I so agree:

If I am in sickness, my sickness may serve Him. If I am in sorrow, my sorrow may serve Him. He does nothing in vain; He knows what He is about.

And I only want to be about the only thing that matters in this world . . . Him!

Let me add, if you're reading this today and your heart is hurting, troubled, or sad by loss, hopelessness, lack of direction, or lack of peace, please take a minute right now. Close your eyes and whisper a little prayer to the only One who can give true peace. Don't be stuck or discouraged. Don't live in regret. When the world seems uncertain, anchor yourself to the only One who is certain: the God of the universe, who loves you dearly and holds you in His hand!

NINETEEN

WORKING THROUGH
THE PRACTICALS

I ignored David's garage for four and a half months.

I couldn't open the door, look at it, or have anything to do with it. It was irrational, I know, but it's how I felt. The garage was David's domain, the place he'd spent many an hour tinkering on cars or sanding wood for a project. Two weeks after the Rainy Day I had to go to his side of the garage to get a screwdriver. It felt like opening Pandora's box—and God only knew what craziness would swirl out from the garage and suck me inside if I did go there.

I know it's silly, impractical, and gives power to a crazy thought that I should have been taking captive instead (2 Corinthians 10:5). But remember, this is how a grieving heart processes. It's really hard to explain and even harder to understand. That's why I keep emphasizing this: if you are at this place or someone you love is, remain loving and really, really gentle with your broken, grieving heart or the grieving hearts of others.

Fortunately, I really didn't have to go into David's side of the garage very often. Our condo had split garages: mine on one side and David's on the other. Unless I had an occasional need for a hammer or screwdriver, I didn't have to enter his side of that garage. I think this is what overshadowed that whole area: these were David's tools I had to rummage through. It just didn't seem right. He should be there with me, either picking out the right tool for me or doing the job himself. Many of our upstairs chores were left undone because I didn't want to go into that garage.

One day, leafing through a mail order magazine, I came across a pink tool set with various sizes and types of screwdrivers, a hammer, a tape measure, and a wrench or two, all in a beautiful, feminine hot pink case. I ordered ten that day! One was for me, and the others were going to be for every widow, new bride, or graduating senior girl I would come across in the next few years. Irrational? Maybe. But for me it was practical. Life doesn't always make sense to others like it does for the one who's experienced loss.

My healthy recovery was going to be much more likely if others just gave me the space I needed for my wacky notions and ideas.

Honestly, personal pain can be so unpredictable that it can make the folks walking the path of grief with you uncomfortable. I think I became inconvenient for some who were closest to me. I don't think they knew what to do with me year after year. I don't blame them. A grieving person doesn't think logically. Our brains don't think the way those of normal people do. Right or wrong, we tend to *think* through our pain. It's hard to articulate unless you've gone through it. The person seems so normal on one level, and they actually are. But on another level, they are dealing with deep, dark hopelessness and despair.

The irrational side of grief doesn't last forever. Give a person time to grieve the way he or she needs to, not the way you think they should. Because, quite honestly, we really don't have a clue as to what the other person is going through. Even if you have experienced loss, even similar loss, all people are different. Your loss isn't the same as another person's. It's not helpful in any way to say, "I know what you're going through." That's an immediate turnoff. When someone started their words to me with that sentence, I immediately either zoned out or thought, *What an idiot!* (Yes, I know, a very ungodly thought. I've asked forgiveness.) Do you know I had a friend who actually compared the loss of selling her house of fifteen years with the loss of my husband? Really? Are you kidding me? I was shocked at her insensitivity, but later felt sorry for her.

I also didn't want to hear that someone knew what I was going through because they'd experienced divorce! No, you *don't* know, and it's not the same kind of loss. It's loss, but not the same. My advice is that you don't compare your loss, especially in the early stages of grief, as you may start your friend into a mental tailspin!

You know, it's interesting, because many widows I've spoken with, years after their loss, would say that the rejection of divorce is probably worse in some ways, because our husbands didn't choose to leave us. I agree: rejection would certainly be an added layer of disappointment, frustration, sadness, and anger on top of grief. I don't doubt that it would be extremely hard to work through. But here is the point I have learned: I don't ever tell a divorced person, "I know what you're going through." Because, even with all of the loss I have experienced, I *don't* know what they're going through!

Condolences that made me feel loved, spoke to my heart, or offered genuine sympathy were usually those coming from one of two groups: folks who also had said good-bye to spouses, and folks who had said good-bye to children. First off, they never said, "I know what you're going through," because they knew they didn't. They knew that, while they too had been at the bottom of the well of deep sorrow, membership in these groups is quite different for everyone. Again, the loss may be similar, but it is not the same. No one will grieve like you do. Even those of you in grief right now, reading this, will surely grieve differently. You aren't supposed to handle or deal with your grief like anyone else. Instead of advice, or clichés, choose instead to give a grieving person love, compassion, and acceptance. Something like, "I'm just so sorry for your loss." Or, "I am praying for you and your family." These things will be honest, fine, and enough.

I love the movie *Lars and the Real Girl*. It resonates with me in such a deep place. Lars is an adult son whose mother died while delivering him in childbirth. His grieving father completely shut down and offered no support for Lars or his older brother. They muddle through life with gaping wounds and hardened hearts. The movie begins with the lives of the brothers as adults, after dad is gone. Lars has a job and lives in the garage apartment next to the house passed down to the boys from their parents. The older brother and his compassionate, lovely, and pregnant wife live in the main house.

Lars develops a delusion to cope with the pain of his loss. The most uncomfortable aspect of Lars's delusion is an anatomically correct blow-up doll he believes to be a real girl. The movie focuses on how this small, loving Wisconsin community does its part to help Lars and his family work through his obvious mental problem. There are many poignant as well as laugh-out-loud funny moments in the movie. The unconditional support and compassion shown by both the small church congregation and townspeople are incredibly touching. In one scene, a meeting in the church basement evolves into a very hard discussion. Members wonder what Lars is thinking. Some ask: "How are we to treat *her*, as a *real* girl?" An older church member interrupts the discussion. "Oh for Heaven's sake! What's the big deal?" Another muddles under his breath, "Well, he won't bring her to church." The pastor sighs deeply, clears his throat, and says, "The question is, as always, what would Jesus do?"[5]

The body of Christ could learn a valuable lesson in kingdom living from this Hollywood flick. No doubt, Jesus would show love.

To me, that's what life in the kingdom is about. It's Scripture. It's pure, unbiased reality with no judgment, no condemnation, no name-calling. We meet hurting, wounded, and, yes, sick people exactly where they are and love them back to life. We can actually partner with God to love people so unconditionally that it becomes life-giving to them. We breathe the breath of restoration, wholeness, health, and joy, and in so doing, we have the privilege to love those struggling back to life. Isn't that lovely? To be on a rescue team whose tools aren't of this world, but contain all the help the hurting ones need. Love. The Beatles got it right on this one: all we need is love. People in the throes of personal pain need patience, kindness, protection, hope, and love. A quick study of 1 Corinthians 13:4-8 shows us what true love looks like. It never fails.

So love people in pain, right where they are! Encourage and pray for them, but don't try to fix them. God is fixing them, and He does all things well.

I use music as an escape. Through my grief, I played all kinds of music, all day and sometimes all night. In this season of grief, I played songs from my high school years as well as songs that breathed life and hope into me. One particularly meaningful song to me is by Darlene Zschech, a worship leader from Australia. The song, "All Things Are Possible," moved me deeply in this particular part of my journey. As soon as I heard it, this phrase rushed in and literally swept me away:

*"You fill my life with greater joy as I delight myself in You."*⁶

I sang that song at the top of my voice for just under an hour one day. I let the words wash over me and sink deeply into every fiber of my being. I wanted so desperately to find joy again. I wanted to be happy, peaceful, and content. I wanted to believe that with God all things are possible, including filling my life with not only joy, once again, but as Zschech sings about: *"greater* joy!" Wow! Could that be true? Is it possible to reach out so far as to grasp *more* joy, even a greater measure than I'd already experienced in my first forty-four years? And then I began to realize: Why not?

I prayed, right then: "God, I'm asking for greater joy. I've been pretty happy in my life up to this point. I've experienced the love of a good man and marriage for twenty-two years, the birth of two wonderful children, and the kindness of others, more than I could ever imagine in a lifetime. But now, Father, at the lowest moments I've ever known and in tremendous sorrow, I'm asking you to fill my life with greater joy as I delight myself in you! Oh Lord, if this is possible, I want it! Give me more life, more joy, more peace, more of everything you have to offer! What is it, God, that your Word says: exceedingly, abundantly, and far more than I can ask or imagine. [See Ephesians 3:20 for the reference.] Yes, God, that's what I want! That's what I'm asking you for! In Jesus' name and for His glory! Amen!"

* * * * * * *

Life moves on, and by this time in our journey, we had something to celebrate! Aubrey and Bradley became engaged! That sweet boy asked to bring me lunch one day, and he said he wanted to visit for a while. I hadn't even thought about what might be coming, but after lunch, he started a turn in the conversation. "Well, I guess I always expected to be driving down to the Saturn plant and having this lunch with Mr. Hunt, but I guess now I get to ask you . . . " Right about then I clued into what this was about, and I started to tear up! I was happy, excited, and sad, all at the same time; a very odd mix of emotions. How I wished Mr. Hunt was having that burger and fries with Bradley! But David was gone and I was the parent in charge.

Brad coming to ask me for Aubrey's hand in marriage was made easier because of something that had happened two months before the Rainy Day. We had gone to dinner on Aubrey's twentieth birthday. And in the middle of dinner, David said something like: We know you guys are well suited for one another and going to get married someday, and you have our blessing. At this point in the dinner scene you could have automatically inserted Aubrey's shifting eyes and awkward repositioning in her chair! She looked at me as if to say: What in the world? Where is Daddy going with this? We're still just dating . . .

But you know what? Wow! Do I have better understanding today! What a wonderful, unexpected gift and blessing! How I thank God! He was truly going before us and making the crooked places straight! (See Isaiah 45:2 for this reference.)

It's true, life goes on. . . . And life was moving forward to new and good times. But still, they were times without David. And now, just thinking about that, I'm sad again . . .

TWENTY

~~When Stupid People Say Stupid Things~~

~~When Well-Meaning People Say Stupid Things~~

When People Try to Help, but Don't

Can you tell I'm having a hard time finding the best title for this chapter? My good days were hit-and-miss for several months. Some days were awesome. I breathed deeply and felt like everything, in time, was going to be just fine. But then I'd have a bad day and be right back to heavy grieving and borderline hopelessness.

The uncertainty of each day really wore on me, and sometimes just talking with friends and pondering the issues of life would get me off track. I would entertain discussions on, or wonder to myself, things like: Why do bad things happen to good people? This is an honest question. But I had no business entering into discussions like these.

I don't think God minds our struggles with the harder concepts of our faith. I think it's a beautiful aspect of Christianity and one that compels me to follow Jesus. God came to earth as a man. Jesus walked here, as one of us, constrained by what constrains us, feeling the emotions of what we feel and confronting the issues of the day: hunger, loneliness, sin, and doubt. He did this all while being fully man and fully God, without sin. He is our example of how it can be done, in holiness and strength from our great God. Jesus didn't do anything on His own. He submitted to His Father. John 5:19 gives us a peek into that relationship. And we do nothing apart from our Father. We are one with Him. He lives inside of us through His Holy Spirit. That's so good, so comforting. We are not alone!

* * * * * * *

Out of the blue, several months after the Rainy Day, I was visiting friends in another city. I woke up early and came out for coffee. My friend's husband was awake, and we started visiting about my journey and all I'd been through since David's accident. I finished talking. He looked at me quizzically and said, "Julie, what you're saying isn't what the Bible teaches. God will keep all believers safe. His Word says so, and if believers die tragically, or too soon, then Satan must have sneaked in somehow and stolen them away. Your family got robbed!"

Whoa! Was that out of the blue! Try hearing that from a well-meaning friend in your first year of grief. I was a little shocked and pretty sure I'd misheard him, so I didn't freak out and listened to him carefully explain his point. I asked him a few questions, mainly for clarification, because I was still having a hard time believing that he'd actually said what I thought I'd heard. To say my head was spinning and my wounded heart hurting even more is a gross understatement.

Did this man just say what I think he said? I sat there asking myself. *Did he just imply—no, explicitly tell me—that David died because Satan sneaked in and snatched him away?*

I was wondering: *Did he hear what I had told him?* Did he listen to my beautiful story, how I have a loving Father, who knew a tragic circumstance was coming and had done so many things, *for years*, so it could be bearable and right with our precious family? Did this man hear me talk about how this whole thing was so covered in prayer, and God's restoring fingerprints were all over it, and how God had made it really, really clear that no man lives forever and . . . well, I wanted to throw up.

The short answer to each of the questions spinning through my mind was a simple: yes. Yes, he did hear it all. He didn't miss a thing, and he rendered his judgment anyway. His veneered understanding of widowhood was apparently so deep and knowledgeable that he had the guts to tell me, in his calm, pastoral voice, how it all was. A man who would never know what widowhood was like, who had not seen his children draped over their dead father's body pleading with God to restore his life, was telling me how it all was. I was stunned. My heart felt attacked, even brutalized. I was like a woman with her hands lifted up, shielding her face from the deadly blows.

The damage was done. He was in and out in less than five minutes. His weapons were his shallow, ill-informed words, and they cut as deep as a machete. He didn't know the hurt he caused at the time, and probably doesn't to this day. I was devastated, but tried to go on with the morning as if nothing had ever happened. I started pushing that wound down deeply to make sure it would never see the light of day again. His wife woke up and we all went to lunch—his treat, of course—and I continued the mind-numbing activities of my day.

The damage he inflicted that day rotted in my soul for the next four years. It didn't need to, but at the time I just didn't have the tools to understand what had happened to me and how to deal with it. What he said boiled down to this: David is gone because you and the children didn't pray hard enough. The church folks praying at the hospital didn't do enough to tip God's healing hand—and you lost. Sorry about that! What a pile of you-know-what! Believe me, I have had to walk in supernatural grace and forgiveness on this one, and my Father has supplied it to the full. But let me describe to you the toll it took on my heart and how the enemy had a field day unleashing the demonic lies that I believed for years. The damage was extensive to my heart. I got stuck in my grief, even falling backward in lies and confusion. I became my own protector and went on an alternate journey that God never intended for me to take.

The steps back to freedom took courage and a lot of work. God had to renew my mind. I had to believe that He is greater than the lie I had chosen to believe. I had to break the power the lie held over me; I had to identify it, renounce it, and break it with the truth of God's Word so He could come rescue me from the demonic attack. Freedom was mine in Christ, but it took a renewed mind and heart to walk it all out. As best as I can understand, when I heard his words that cut so deep, the grieving, wounded part of me, which couldn't bear the attack, broke off from the stronger me and hid in the recesses of my being. I couldn't entertain the possibility that his words might be true, so I ran from them. The stronger Julie came out as a protector, taking over the mind and directing the wounded parts to hide from the lies until it was safe to come out again. The stronger Julie is the one who made the decision not to argue with him, but instead to cut ties and run.

Stronger Julie also emerged, later, to take the reins and lead me back out into the world to recover and get on with life. She was the guardian, the keeper of all things. "Nothing more will happen to you on my watch, sweetie," she seemed to be saying. "I got your back. I'll see to it that nothing like this conversation ever happens again. This strong Julie will take such attentive care to Cameron and Aubrey and their needs that nothing—nothing!—bad will ever happen to us again!"

This may sound heroic and good, but the problem is I was never designed to carry my own burdens. Jesus makes it clear *He's* the burden-carrier. As my well-intentioned self emerged, I took on a number of ungodly beliefs, including that I was the master and commander of my destiny. I was now the protector of my life and my loved one's lives. Maybe our family had messed up in the past, and for a fleeting moment, I wondered if God had forgotten us. I will see to it and become super-mommy, super-friend, super-daughter, and super-grieving widow! I played each and every part so very well that I even fooled myself! Remember how strong I told you I was before the accident? Well, I totally fell back into those old habits. Good, strong, capable Julie. The one folks knew and admired. I would just put my mask back on and get on with life. I actually remember thinking there's no other way out. I have to do better because when I don't, people die. Daddies die.

At times I honestly wondered if *these days* would be my breaking point. The cruelest incident of my life, sending me over the edge and past the point of no return, wouldn't be the Rainy Day, but the years after it. What a paradox! On one hand, I tried so very hard to be a good Christian widow, and on the other hand, I was a wounded, fragile woman that I barely knew. Maybe it was so hard for me to understand because I'd always been such a strong, capable, determined, pull-yourself-up-by-your-bootstraps kind of gal. But in these days, I couldn't find my boots or their straps! I didn't even know where to look. And now this kick in the teeth from a clueless brother in Christ.

Oh, the wasted years this ungodly belief stole from me, and with my consent! I was a wounded soldier shot by a fellow soldier; this was friendly fire! How sad and tragic! Our enemy does not play fair! If he can keep you away from God through unbelief, he wins. In Jesus Christ we are born again believers. We are redeemed, and the transformation/sanctification process begins. However, if the enemy can sow seeds of doubt, confusion, unbelief, jealousy—and more—in fertile ground of the soil of our hearts, those seeds can take root and grow. His plan then is to render you useless *inside* the kingdom of God. You may have eternity with Jesus guaranteed, but the enemy wants to make sure you don't bring anyone else with you. Your "wounded warrior" status will become a crippling lifestyle that breeds death, not life. That's exactly what the enemy set out to accomplish in me. I got off track and started making my own plans, believing the enemy's lies and empowering him! I almost sabotaged my journey of grief by just stuffing it, moving on, and not fully dealing with my pain. I was so tired of all of the heartache, trying so hard and still hurting. *God, can I just move on with life, be a mom to Aubrey and Cameron, and find my new way?*

So, at this point, weak, wounded, and hurting Julie stayed down in the trenches, while strong Julie emerged out of the hole with her cape of courage and determination to go on with life, whether she felt healed or not. Life goes on, right? *And I better just go along with it,* I told myself, *because folks need me.*

Pam's cancer had come back with a vengeance that first summer after the Rainy Day. About six weeks after the one-year anniversary of David's relocation to Heaven, I walked Pam to the end of the road and said good-bye to her. It hurt so much; it was sorrow upon sorrow! I'm convinced the only way I survived that loss was to stuff my pain even further down! I really didn't know what to do but keep functioning and pray I wasn't found out.

My kids were coping and life was moving on and even bringing some good things. Cameron was starting his sophomore year of football and would probably get to play as an underclassman, which was a big deal at his school. Aubrey was about to marry Brad, the man of her dreams. Cameron would walk her down the aisle, and all of our family and friends would gather again for a much happier occasion.

TWENTY-ONE

THE UNEXPECTED ANSWER TO MY PRAYERS

Hope: It smiles from the threshold of the year to come,
Whispering, 'It will be happier . . . '

—ALFRED TENNYSON

The only explanation I have for this chapter of my life is that God is good and kind. He knows our hearts and what we need. I remember praying two specific prayers early on, during the period in which I felt so afraid and alone.

One: "God, please don't make me be on the dating scene. I was so horrible at dating the first time around. I never, never thought I'd have to do this again. *God! Please, have mercy on me! Please God, I'm asking you for this one thing.* My humble request is this: please let my lips kiss only one other man besides David. I'm asking you that the next man who kisses my lips . . . please God, let him be the one."

Two: "*God, whoever comes into my life is going to have to have a really, really big heart.* I mean, it's got to be big enough for me, Aubrey, Cameron, and David. I know it's silly, God, but David's got to come with me into this new life that I believe you have for me. Please, God. I know you can do … really great things. Impossible things."

These were the two things I prayed consistently. So simple, almost childlike, and with a hint of Disney, you know? "A dream is a wish your heart makes." Widowhood had humbled me. I was so scared and yet I trusted God. I was so afraid. I was so young and I didn't want to be alone for the rest of my life!

What did God do? He sent a wonderful, kind, and godly man to me about halfway through the first year of my loss. While we met that first year, we didn't start dating until a couple of months after the one-year anniversary of David's relocation. Kye had experienced an unwanted divorce after twenty-four years of marriage. He was broken and recovering when we met. He too had been going through the steps of a different kind of grief, trying to piece life together again. We talked on the phone from July through the next April. Our conversations were mainly about how much I missed David and how much he missed his family! We shared life stories, laughed, cried, and found much common ground in our faith, college football, and a deep desire to live again. I was a bit uneasy, thinking that if Kye in fact was the one, God had sent him a little too soon, because I was a wreck and in the most vulnerable time of my life.

But when Kye came into my life, things became different. He helped me in my grieving process. God used him to help me believe I could live again. I missed talking with David so much, and Kye helped me transition through that loss. We talked a lot on the phone, sharing our heartache over loss and our deep desire to see God restore the years the locusts had eaten. (Joel 2:25 is a great reference for this concept.)

I remember hanging up the phone some evenings saying, "Oh my, if he's the one, I'm not sure he'll stay around. This is not how the beginning of a relationship should go! All I talked about was David! What's wrong with me? What is this guy thinking? I bet I'll get the big send-off soon, like 'Hey, crazy woman! Get your life together before you even *think* about dating or marriage!'"

Believe me, I would never advocate for making such an important decision so soon after such a devastating loss. I mean, don't the experts say to wait something like three to seven years before you date or get married? Good Lord, help me, sweet Jesus!

Somehow, it was right for us. When we finally did start dating, fourteen months after the Rainy Morning, I felt like I was in junior high again—only making really good decisions this time! Kye is handsome, kind, charming, and funny! I was falling so quickly in love with this man that I couldn't believe it. He seemed to really care for me too. He told me he'd never before felt the way he felt about me. He said I was pretty, and he admired my deep faith in God. He also told me he was so sorry for what I had been through the previous year, and that I was open to cry or talk about it as much as I wanted or needed to.

And my kids loved him. My family and friends thought he was the cutest and sweetest guy they'd ever met. My sister-in-law Jone told me that she'd been praying since the Rainy Day that God, in His timing, would send a really special man for me to walk with the rest of my life.

His family was delighted in me and happy to see Kye living life again. The folks I cared about the most, second to my kids, were those in David's family. His mom and sister both gave us two thumbs way up! It was so beautiful and honoring to have them say, "We trust God and we trust you, Julie." They never once made me feel ashamed for marrying so soon. They never said an unkind word or insinuated anything negative. They welcomed Kye with open arms, and they still do to this day! I'm teary-eyed just thinking about what a gift that is to us.

And my prayers? Oh, no doubt, they were answered. I showed the video of David's life to Kye only a month after we officially started dating. I didn't cry when we watched it. I'd guess I'd seen it too many times to shed more tears. But Kye? He cried like a baby! I asked him why. "Why are you crying? You didn't even know David." His answer? "What a great man and what a great life! I'm sorry I never got to meet him, and I'm so sorry for what you and the kids have had to walk through!" *Wow!*, I thought. *Answer to prayers? Done!*

And about that first kiss . . . I was very concerned because I knew that if our phone conversations became in-person conversations, I would be super vulnerable. So, when our relationship changed, I set down some house rules. Something like: Don't touch me! No hugs, side or otherwise, and certainly no kissing. I'm not going to kiss you because I have no idea where this is going. He was very understanding and appropriate.

About two months into dating, we kissed . . . and then I knew. God *had* sent the one to me, and I'd never have to kiss another! We knew we had a lot of hard work ahead of us, putting our two families of four adult children, two teenagers, and one granddaughter into one big happy family. It hasn't been easy, and some days we aren't as successful as we'd like to be, but we've always done everything with love in action.

* * * * * * *

We married January 1, 2006, one month before the two-year anniversary of the Rainy Day. Kye has been the best husband for my second chance at life. I'm so glad that, even in my wounded state, I was given an opportunity to love, and God outdid Himself with Kye.

Unfortunately, some people make a bad assumption. They believe that when a grieving person marries again, the grief is over and he or she is on to a wonderful new life. Well, yes and no. I was happy, in love, and beginning a new life.

But I was also a broken, grieving woman who needed to engage life carefully until I was mended, whole, and revived.

Part Two

TWENTY-TWO

HAND OVER THE BURDEN (SO NO ONE ELSE GETS HURT)

So here I was. On one hand, I was happy. It had been more than five years since the Rainy Morning. I'd started a new life with a wonderful man. Aubrey had finished a master's degree and was a happily married bride. Cameron was a missionary in Sweden, Cambodia, and Thailand. Life was sweet and good, and from all outside appearances, the kids and I had survived the Rainy Day.

But from an emotional standpoint? I was surviving, remaining alive, and getting through, but not thriving—not by a long shot. I was like a weak, fragile, undernourished plant. In some ways, I was miserable. I felt anxious, like just waiting for the other shoe to drop. It was almost as though I couldn't accept that life could be good or even easy now. Something else was bound to happen, right? There's no way I could have

gotten through this entire ordeal, right? Because, in all my experiences, something else *always* happens. How nice it would
have been for someone, like a referee, to walk on the scene and
call a time-out or throw a yellow penalty flag. The call might
be: "False start—believing lies from Satan!" Can we replay this
from prayer's ending, Lord? I want to experience greater joy
again. Yep, that would have saved me a few years of floating
adrift in the sea. But remember, I had become my own protector and, basically, I was finally running out of steam.

If I pinpointed the source of my anxiety, it would have cen-
tered around my kids. I was still sad and worried for Cameron;
what if he dies overseas? What if something bad happens to
him and I'm not there to save him? I mean, I'm very happy
he's serving the Lord, but I can't protect him way over there!
This can't be right. Why can't I just trust God to look after
him? And what about Aubrey? Is she really happy? I mean, she
seems to be really happy, but maybe she's just burying herself
in work now, or maybe she's mad at me. Did I do something or
say something that hurt her? She seems to be shutting me out
a little bit. Help me, Jesus! No one would've ever known about
the chaos swirling through my mind because I was a master
at wearing the mask. From the outside, I appeared happy and
fine. After all, wasn't I supposed to be happy by now? I mean,
I'd walked through this right, hadn't I?

Transparent about grief? Check.

Open and honest about my feelings? Check.

Remarried and now happy? Maybe.

I mean, I was married to the most fabulous man in the
world, right? Seriously, what would be the major malfunction
that would keep me from leaping on the happy train and letting it carry me away? But the continuing struggle was real.
Just another view into the messy world of grief. I couldn't bear
for anyone to think that I'd taken my grieving mess and made
it worse, not better! That would be a huge faux pas! Shame was

pressing hard on my heart and, once again, the mess called my life was disappointing and ugly. There was a gnawing feeling that the flashing neon sign I imagined over my head, the one with the word *Widow* on it, had new words up there in lights: *General Screw-Up.*

Shame can twist your thoughts and tie you up in knots so very quickly. I could be a strong, godly woman, trusting and believing in God one moment. And then, minutes later, a thought, a word, a phone call, or a picture could draw me back into the doubt, despair, and hopelessness I knew so well.

JOURNAL, JANUARY 7, 2009

I am encouraging myself in the Lord today. I delight myself in Him. He can do ALL things and he does all things so well. I will dwell on the good things in my life today: my health, Kye's health, and my home. I feel sort of a paralyzing grip from the Lord today. A grip so firm, so fast, that I cannot escape, even if I want to. A grip holding so tightly! I'm in complete peace, although everything around me is crashing in. I feel like I should do something, but there's nothing to do. No guidance, no direction . . . have I missed something? Should I be doing something? And then: . . . silence . . . long silence . . . mind-maddening silence. . . . Finally, I begin writing again. What will people think? I'm messing up. I'm racing from thought to thought . . .

A thought breaks into my madness: Trust me, child. Trust me. I cry out to God: "You are the only one worth having! I give you my all today, God. You are my only hope! Thank you in advance for coming through for me, sorting out all of the ins and outs of my life!"

Again, I cannot stress how successful I was at hiding! No one would have guessed I was holding on by a mere thread. But the good news is the thread was from the garment of Jesus!

In hindsight, these were, perhaps, some of my hardest days of grief. I think I tried so hard to get Aubrey and Cameron out of the hole of grief that when I finally stopped and looked around, I realized: *Hey, where is everybody? I'm still in the hole!* The honest assessment? I was collapsing under the weight of my grief. I expect that you know from experience that hurts we try to deny or hide away have a way of making themselves known.

I was miserable, hurting, and facing a choice: continue living in the pit with the lies and pain, or start climbing out. Choose one more time to let the burdens go and give them *all* to the One so perfectly suited to carry them. The One who'd already accomplished everything I needed at the cross—and gave it to me freely! Swimming lessons while drifting in the sea were over. I saw the waters part and decided to walk through. Even though I had gotten so far off track, God's loving arms were not too short to reach down and save me one more time! Besides, months were going by quickly, and now Aubrey was expecting her first child and I needed to be well for her, the baby, and myself.

I reached out to a friend who knew me well and was trustworthy. I needed someone who was mature and could listen thoughtfully to my aching heart. I hadn't told anyone except Kye and David *everything* about me, ever. It was a huge, vulnerable moment that I welcomed with open arms, for I was exhausted! I was like a stuck pig, pouring out years of pain, heartache, and anguish as I pulled off every mask, revealing the lost little girl named Julie. But looking back, I think the trauma was stuffed so far down that I needed extra help.

Little did I know, this friend had taken classes that year in trauma therapy. The Holy Spirit gave her insight on how to probe and pry open a crack to let love in and pain out. I talked and she listened, thoughtfully asking questions about my journey. At one point, she said, "Tell me about that friend you mentioned a minute ago. I believe he's a pastor?" I spilled the details and she listened. She ministered love, truth, and hope to me that afternoon. I'll spare you the gory details of our sessions, but in short, my two Julies were reunited as I called forth the weaker, hurting Julie from the dark place to which I had assigned her. Strong, self-sufficient Julie humbled herself, repented, and took her rightful place alongside the still grieving and wounded Julie. Together, they lay on the living room sofa, closed their eyes, and started addressing the grief work that was left to be done.

I asked the only healer, Jesus, to come back to the scene of the damage to my heart: the living room of the pastor-friend. I replayed the entire scene, asking questions, this time directly to Jesus.

"Jesus, when he said those things to me, where were you? Where were you in the room, Jesus?" The whole process took more than an hour and I even fell asleep during part of it. But when I awoke, I still had the question on my lips, even if I was a bit groggy: "Jesus, where were you?"

I heard, as clearly as anything I've ever heard, a voice saying: *I was right there, Julie. I was holding you, cushioning the painful blows from the words too brutal to be the truth.* Wow! I woke up quickly, amazed at what I had just heard! I tuned in deeper, listening still. *"The facts are this, Julie. You and the kids did everything just the way I wanted you to on February 5th, 2004. You didn't miss or forget a thing! You walked everything out so beautifully and I am so very proud of you! You have trusted me in the midst of tragedy and I have been with you the whole time. I've never left your side and I will never leave your side. This man was wrong. He was wrong in what he said and in the way he said it. He's wrong in what he believes and how he treated you. He is a wounded child and his own heart needs healing. He is my child, Julie, just as you are my child. I will teach him when he is ready. But you must forgive him, Julie. I want you to pray for him too. He's working very hard to keep it all together. He needs to let go.*

It was not hard for me to forgive him, especially when I saw him as Jesus saw him: a weak, wounded soldier who needed his own healing from the Father. I wanted for him what I was receiving myself. I was familiar with God's Word enough to know this: holding onto bitterness, judgment, anger, or unforgiveness wouldn't affect him, but it certainly would affect me! Allowing any of that rotten seed to remain in me would wreak more havoc, crippling me and rendering me useless in the kingdom of life! I'd just been invited to freedom and wholeness. I had no intention of crossing back into prison. And my heavenly Father had no intention of letting me go there either. All I had to do was say yes. Yes to life, yes to living, yes to hope, and yes to Jesus, every single day.

Jesus managed this part of the journey: the pace we walked, where we stopped, how we unloaded baggage, and when we reached our destination. My only requirements were to surrender to Him each morning and trust Him completely to finish the good work He and I began. That was great revelation. I've tried so hard my entire life to get it right, be a good girl, and make my parents, teachers, God, Jesus—everyone—happy and proud of my choices. It was really refreshing to find, out of this tremendous loss, pain, and heartache, that Jesus wanted to carry all of my burdens and transform me so I could be a living sacrifice! I remember thinking: *this is really good news!* But I soon realized: *hey, this is great news!* And isn't that exactly what the gospel is?

For the first time in a long time, I was excited about life. I felt like a door was opened and I was given the chance to crawl out of the darkness and into the light! I was five years into my journey when this new freedom came. I have developed such an appreciation for the grieving process as a distance race. I won't ever try to hurry anyone through it.

TWENTY-THREE

KEEPING MY HEART BETWEEN THE LINES OF LOVE

Our trials, our sorrows, and our grieves develop us.

—ORISON SWETT MARDEN

Hope deferred makes the heart sick.

—PROVERBS 17:22

Julie's version of that verse: Heartbreak, disappointment, and weariness will rot away at your bones and make you physically ill.

Ever dream of a new beginning, a wonderful fresh start? Ever wish you could just snap your fingers, disappear from the life you live, and step into the life you want? Me too! And that's exactly what I did.

In 2009 I hit the restart button on my life.

In January the typical calls to action begin: new year, new beginning, lose weight, start exercising, get out of the hole you're stuck in, and on and on. We're inundated with these calls for change, ad nauseam, but I think they are also what invited me to look at my unfulfilled life, gather a little more courage and, once again, do something different.

What's that definition of stupid? Doing the same thing over and over and expecting something to change? Well, I've never fancied myself as stupid, so I started paying better attention to those longings of my heart, those areas that I needed to get unstuck, so I could make efforts to move on.

Back to cold January, sitting in my big comfy chair. Morning after morning I began to unravel the tightly woven garment I had constructed to keep my pain out and a shoddy form of survival in. Threads of disappointment, sadness, even bitterness gave the signals of unmanaged pain. It was like the other side of the coin. On the flip side I was doing OK, but God was interested in bringing His healing power to the underside of the coin, the side I was neatly hiding under layers of brokenness. I was distancing myself between friendships of the past. My heart was tender and my brain overloaded from pain. Friendships were difficult to maintain. Life was hard to live. Simple conversations could easily be misinterpreted and throw me into confusion or depression. Not being included in social events hurt deeply. I felt as though I needed an interpreter just to communicate with friends and sometimes family. I took offense to many things others said and did. The confusion caused my head and heart to put up walls to keep me safe. It was ugly, and the pain took me into a journey from which I didn't know how to escape.

What I've learned, on this side of grief, is to stay before the Lord until all the tender places are fully healed. By doing this, I was able to emerge in the peace and joy my heavenly Father had for me. It meant pulling back a bit from life and regrouping. I learned how to set healthy boundaries with family and friends. The unhealed Julie, the one emerging from the merry-go-round of life, had made some poor decisions that led to unhealthy relationships. Instead of desperately spinning around, in an attempt to make life easier, better, happier, and more abundant, I decided to do a courageous thing: I would get off the ride and close the whole park down! Yes, the enemy had stolen precious time from me. I had many regrets from living in the hole of grief and despair, and the price was too high to participate in this game any longer. It had already cost me a great deal, and I wasn't interested in paying one more thin dime. God brought me new friendships and strengthened old ones. And I was already beginning to understand the most valuable re-directive: That He is with me and He will never leave me!

According to God's Word, every morning brings new mercies. (See Lamentations 3:22, 23 for a great reference.) There was no need to look in the past. If this were indeed a season of new choices, I would choose now to live in the day, in the moment, and start dreaming about my future again. My focus shifted from my problems and circumstances to my answers and hope, both of which are found in Jesus.

I continued talking with Him throughout my day, like He was in the room with me, but one January morning was different. I wasn't the desperate widow begging for peace. I wasn't the new bride living from behind a curtain of imagined shame. No, this morning I was a *daughter*. A daughter not orphaned, but dearly loved. A daughter newly plucked from the hole of despair, encouraged by hope, and learning to walk with a renewed mind. My Savior, Jesus, would take my pain so I wouldn't have to wear it like my grandma wore her broach, front and center on a clean polyester suit. A key element in my recovery was understanding that I had to surrender the pain, not surrender to the pain. I had to turn off all the imaginary, invisible neon signs above my head (remember "Widow" and "General Screw-Up"?), once and for all, and refuse to ever pull the chain to turn them on again. I put past tense verbs into my vocabulary. I *was* widowed. I *have gone through* the most painful journey of my life. The pain in my life has gone. And I activated some present tense verbs: I *am* healed. I *feel* joy. I *am loved* by so many.

I can honestly embrace love in the present because when I made the decision to take the neon signs down, God answered another prayer of my heart: "Give me a revelation of your love, Father God." I wanted Him, the living God, my Father, to be a Father *to me*. I wanted to be His daughter and let Him know the real me. I wanted Him to reveal His heart to me; I wanted to know what He was like, what He thinks. I wanted to spend time in His presence and hear, firsthand, just how much He loves me. I was laying down the old me, the one in which I pictured myself as an orphan child, the one who thought she had to fend for herself, even protect herself. I threw my head back on the cushion of my soft, comfy chair and said, "God, reveal yourself anew to me! Your Word says you love me more than I know; show me your glory! Show me your loving kindness. Woo my heart back to believing that you are indeed crazy about me."

I went through the next few days enjoying life and finding pleasure in the little gifts He gives. I found myself talking with Him and feeling impressions of His speaking back to me. I asked Him to show me how much He loves me, to actually give me not just a revelation of His love, but a *revolution*—something like a forcible overthrow of government or social order (in this case, the old rules of my heart) in favor of a new system! Yes! I knew the old order of my life had been vanquished, and I wanted the new regime to stand guard and help me protect the ground I'd just recovered. I needed a fresh revelation of the Father's love for me. I needed to know that

God the Father is my daddy, and all He requires from me is to be His daughter. Let me say that again . . . I needed to know that God the Father is my daddy, and all He requires from me is to be His daughter. He's not mad at me, He's not disappointed with me, He doesn't think I'm a big screw-up . . . He just loves me! That's it. That's all! It's simple, yet profoundly life changing *and* life giving.

Instantly, that kind of mind-set gets rid of all my performance issues. My striving, my perfectionism, my controlling, and my believing that I have to do it all myself is gone! That's freedom! All I have to do is believe and trust Him! That's it. So simple. And guess what? It also answers all my questions of what I'm supposed to be doing with my life because all I'm required to do is be like Jesus. I spend time with my Father; I see what He's doing and join Him! That is the foundation of kingdom living. We spend time with the Father and do what He's doing, which looks an awful lot like loving people.

This was wonderful head knowledge, but our Father God always has more. His greatest desire is for me, His daughter, to move this knowledge from my head to my heart and let it transform me. God is true to His Word, growing me beyond myself! I was learning how to grow with Christ. My flesh was being squeezed and it did not feel good. I am selfish, and God was calling me on it!

One day—yet again—I was at the end of my rope. I yelled out to God: "It's so hard loving people when they're so rotten! I can't do this! God! I can't love these people. I don't know how! I need a revelation of your love. I need you to do something radical to show me how much you love me and how I can give that love away to others!"

TWENTY-FOUR

YOU GET WHAT YOU ASK FOR

Three days later, in my kitchen, scurrying around as I do, I noticed the clock on the microwave. It said: 10:10. I thought to myself, *That's odd. The numbers are the same.* And instantly I remembered I'd looked at the bedroom clock early that morning at 4:44. I didn't give it much more thought and went on with my day.

After lunch, I glanced at the clock and it said: 1:11. *Whoa! That is weird.* And at 3:33, when I just happened to look at the clock once again, I cried out in disbelief: "What is going on here?" Immediately, I had the deepest knowing within my heart: "Julie, you asked me for a tangible way for you to know I love you. This is it. I love you so much that I want to tell you all the time. So, every time you look at a clock and it has the numbers the same, that's me telling you, 'I love you!'"

I was blown away! "What is happening to me? This is crazy. God, is this really you? Is this really happening to me?"

"Julie, I want you to know, through all the heartache, pain, and hurt you've gone through, that I'm here, I'm with you. I never left. I love you and I want you to be sure of it. I love you so very much, and I want to tell you. I want you to know it from the top of your head right down to your heart."

At first I felt like a young girl with a big crush! Like I had this secret boyfriend who was passing notes to me in class. And yet, it went deeper than that. He was pursuing me. And I was falling for it, falling for Him, the lover of my soul! I cried, but this time not sobbing tears of pain and sorrow; these tears were different. These tears were coming from unbelievable truth. You know when something really, really good happens to you and you're so happy you cry? Right there, in my big comfy chair, the very same place where I used to beg Him to let me live life again, to be happy, to fall in love, and not be alone. I collapsed into His arms and let Him begin to love me back to life. It was like He was caressing me, running His fingers through my hair. I felt so secure. He's always seen me as a beautiful princess, His daughter, but my eyes had been blind to such knowledge, too wonderful for me, too great for me to understand! All the doubt, mistrust, confusion, anger, and sorrow lifted, immediately. I knew what I had seen and what I had heard, and I was forever changed! My journey may have been painful, hard, difficult, and sad, but this line from the song "How He Loves," by John Mark McMillan, rings so true to my heart:

> *"I don't have time to maintain these regrets*
> *when I think about the way . . . He loves us!"*[7]

I printed this song lyric out in a fancy font and put it by my kitchen desk and on the mirror over my vanity. I knew this was the answer to every question of my heart. From now on, all the whats, hows, whos, whens, and whys were answered, revealed to me by a loving God! He loves us! Whoa! How He loves us! And seriously, I don't have time anymore, remembering, sorting out, and taking care of all my regrets, because . . . nothing else matters. He loves us. He loves me!

The clock thing? Well, it has continued, every day, for years. It's still going on, six years later! It's the sweetest thing, and we've had so much fun with it! In the middle of the night . . . 2:22. At midday . . . 12:12. And sometimes He's done variations like 12:34 or the beginning of the phone number of someone I know. And I just smile, laugh, or pray for the person, or all three! It's a fun little activity that I enjoy, and I believe God does too. I've told others about it in hopes they'll increase their faith and ask God to show them, in a tangible way, how much He loves them—because He does! I know He does, and you know what? He loves you like that too! Why don't you ask Him for something like that? I have a friend who gets bombarded with hearts—like they're everywhere! Another friend sees yellow smiley faces and says it's like God telling her, "I love you!" These are all just precious ways a supernatural Father delights and interacts with His children.

* * * * * * *

When our grandson was 12 months old, he'd pick up any hat he saw, put it on his head, and say over and over, "at, at, at!" Of course, we all marveled at how precious and smart he was to do such a thing. But what made it doubly precious was the fact he was imitating his daddy, who likes to wear a baseball cap on weekends. This cherished grandson was observing his daddy, liked what he saw, and wanted to be like him. What do you think that did to my son-in-law's heart? You're exactly right! It melted like a snowball on a warm day! It's the same with our heavenly Father. We melt his heart when He sees us, His kids, trying to be like Him. And even though we do it imperfectly—wearing our "at" sideways or backward—it doesn't matter to Him, because He is looking straight into our hearts, and He loves what He sees!

I am devoting my days to resting, abiding, and learning to stay in that revelation: God loves me. He cares for me deeply and desires to give me good gifts and revelation from His very heart—straight to mine! It's by far the safest and most fun place to live!

I'm About to Get Up has become my reality. I am up from my big comfy chair of pain, loss, and grief and I'm living again. The scripture I had come across four years before the Rainy Day, Micah 7:8, was my new meditation:

Do not gloat over me, my enemy! Though I have fallen, I will arise. Though I sit in darkness, the Lord will be my light.

TWENTY-FIVE

IF YOU DON'T CHANGE, NOTHING WILL CHANGE

*"God only allows pain if He's allowing
something new to be born."*

—ANN VOSKAMP

I knew there was so much more to the relocation, death, loss, and sorrow process. I began to ask God to show me His view of it all. When I think about it, it's kind of a no-brainer: if death is in the Bible, then doesn't that make it part of the plan, part of life? After all, doesn't Solomon, the wisest man in the Bible, write, "For death is the destiny of every man; the living should take this to heart" (Ecclesiastes 7:2)? And then there is this, from Isaiah 57:1, 2:

The righteous perish and no one ponders it in his heart; devout men are taken away and no one understands that the righteous are taken away to be spared from evil. Those who walk up-

rightly enter into peace; they find rest as they lie in death.

I guess it's circling back to what I was going through in an earlier stage, which I described earlier in the chapter "My Unknown Future." I needed my Father to show me more of what He was trying to teach me in the beginning of my journey, before I got so off track. I've been challenged by a nagging thought that leads me down a path I'm not sure I even want to be on. Sounds silly, doesn't it? Logically, I think I've tried to ignore the markers on this path, putting blinders over my eyes or sticking my fingers in my ears, but it's no use. God is trying to get my attention on the subject of death. But what He's trying to connect me to isn't about the sad or hard parts. It's about the beauty of it. How He displays His goodness and glory in such desperate hours. He wanted me to stop fearing the death of a body on earth and see it as the Trinity sees it: beautiful, precious, and exciting! It takes a broad leap of faith to believe He can bring clarity to this wonder and, yes, even display goodness to surround the most tragic moments of our lives. And friends, that's exactly what He wants us to know. He wants us to know that He's with us and can turn *anything* around for our good if we'll let Him and trust Him through the process! Notice the emphasis on: *He's with us.* I don't believe he does these tragic things. I don't believe God ever causes car accidents, cancer, plane crashes, rape, murder, and other terrible occurrences. He never brings tragedy or death to His children's lives. He's the author of life and salvation, not death. He's always good and is for our good. Believe me when I say it took a long time for me to even begin to comprehend these concepts. But what I noticed was that as my own heart experienced deeper healing and understanding of the Father and his love for me, I was able to better understand this extremely important verse.

Such love has no fear, because perfect love expels all fear. If we are afraid, it is for fear of punishment, and this shows that we have not fully experienced his perfect love (1 John 4:18, NLT).

This verse explains it all. When I am afraid, I don't understand the magnitude and greatness of our good God! Perfect love casts out, expels, and gets rid of fear— but whose perfect love is John talking about? For years I thought it was my love, like . . . the more love I had, I would not be fearful. But no, that's not it! The perfect love is *God's perfect love!* His love, which is perfect all the time, in every situation, drives out my fear! I cannot know and understand His perfect love and still remain in fear, bound by chains in life, hard places, and tragic circumstances. When I opened my eyes and heart to the revelation God gave me of His great love for all of His creation, I was overwhelmed! And as I walked in this new revelation, renewing my mind and letting His love transform my heart, I had no room for fear! None. Not an ounce. Not one ounce of fear, worry, doubt, or anxiety! Fear could not coexist in my heart when His love completely inhabited my heart. It's the same way that darkness can't remain when you turn a light on. The light completely overtakes the darkness. It dispels, banishes, eliminates—it just completely gets rid of it!

And you know what I realized? That if I'd seen the goodness of God in the smallest yet grandest of ways, then what if all of this is true? God has hidden many mysteries and is waiting for us to discover them.

If you look for me wholeheartedly, you will find me (Jeremiah 29:13).

I love those who love me, and those who seek me diligently will find me (Proverbs 8:17).

It is the glory of God to conceal a matter; to search out a matter is the glory of kings (Proverbs 25:2).

This is so encouraging, isn't it? God has treasure for His children. If we stay focused on Him and not our problems or circumstances, He will meet us, wipe away our tears, and restore to us what has been stolen!

The New Testament is full of these "search and seek" verses as well. Jesus told stories in parables. The kingdom of God, He would say, is like thus and so. Stories of farmers sowing seed, shepherds looking for lost sheep, and a woman searching frantically for a lost coin. I think there's wisdom here that suggests God likes to hide things for us—so that when we look for and discover those things, we receive joy and He receives glory!

But seek first the kingdom of God and His righteousness, and all these things shall be added to you (Matthew 6:33).

Ask, and it will be given to you; seek, and you will find; knock, and it will be opened to you (Luke 11:9).

God did this so that they would seek him and perhaps reach out for him and find him, though he is not far from any one of us (Acts 17:27).

He is a rewarder of those who diligently seek Him (Hebrews 11:6).

What great news! God has understanding and revelation He is waiting to unfold. For whom? Those who are hungry for it! Those who are desperate for His comfort!

TWENTY-SIX

TREASURE HUNTING WITH MY HEAVENLY FATHER

Do you remember when I wrote in my journal that I was on an adventure, with so much to learn? Well, I didn't know what an understatement that was! God was kind to not unload everything on me that first year, or even the second, third, fourth, or fifth years! His ways are so perfect for our lives. He knows what we need during recovery, and when we need it.

Believe me when I say I didn't choose this path; I really mean it! But I do believe with all my heart that it chose me! Who would choose, as a 10-year-old, to watch their beloved Papa fall back into his son's arms and die? Or, at 15, to have her boyfriend suffer a terrible high-speed crash and be killed instantly? Then, at 23, a phone call and your daddy is gone. No matter that you're carrying your first child. The loss is excruciating. My daddy will never see or hold my daughter! Then Valerie, my best friend, college roommate, fellow radio broadcaster, and mom to the most precious little boy . . . left to get hamburgers and diapers and was never heard from again. The man who kidnapped her was a serial murderer. She was his last victim.

That loss was almost the end of me. I was so young and had no idea how to process all of this grief I was carrying in my young life. So I hid part of my heart away, busying myself with being a wife, a new mother, and starting a new life in Nashville.

Oh God, why so much death with hard, tragic circumstances? And to think I wasn't finished yet! God does have the highest wisdom, to keep life unfolding in front of us, to not give us the complete movie to watch all at once. But perhaps the path to understanding any of life—the good, the bad, and the painful—begins with renewing the mind. To come out of the ache that death causes and come into the light, the truth of what God says about it, and into the understanding that Jesus and the Holy Spirit give to help us make sense of it all. You see, I'd believed, along with many others, that the goal or focus of this life was to stay alive. Isn't it odd that we put so much emphasis on this and spend thousands of dollars on dieting, being healthy, exercising, and going to any extreme to prolong our lives on earth? I get it. I think about staying healthy as well. It's just when you have stared death down, in nearly every decade in your life, it doesn't frighten you anymore. Death is like the Wizard of Oz. He hides behind a curtain and makes you think he's big and powerful. But in truth, he has no sting, no victory. And this is what Paul says in 1 Corinthians 15:57.

Where, O death, is your victory? Where, O death, is your sting?

Having read this far, you know me pretty well. I don't give up easily. I just keep digging and digging. If my heavenly Father has me on this treasure hunt, then I want to reach *all* of the treasure! After heartache upon heartache, I'm searching for jewel after jewel, craving all of His revelation and love for us.

So I keep on going and my search leads me to this question for believers in Jesus Christ: Why do we work so hard to stay here if our goal, our prize, our reward, is in another place? If I truly believe that my citizenship is in Heaven (Philippians 3:20) and my goal is to live with Jesus forever in eternity (John 3:3), why would my focus in life be to stay here as long as humanly possible? And why would leaving here seem like the greatest pain? Why is the death of a believer the saddest thing ever? Especially when, in our minds, it's premature? It's an interesting question, isn't it? Paul addressed this specifically in Romans 12:2, where he wrote about renewing the mind:

*Do not conform to the pattern of this world, but be
transformed by the renewing of your mind.
Then you will be able to test and approve what
God's will is—his good, pleasing and perfect will.*

God made it clear to me that I had to give the burden of my loss to Him and let Him renew my mind in the area of loss and grief. Proverbs 1 and 2 talk a great deal about wisdom and understanding, including what can happen if we reject wisdom. I didn't want to be foolish or unteachable concerning grief, especially when the One who knows best and loves me the most was inviting me to learn more. I would have to make a decision, though. I'd need to throw out most of what I'd believed about death, loss, and life beyond the grave. This clean sweep would allow my Father God to teach me His perspective on these things. As you can imagine, much had to change and become new, including what I thought was the path to healing and wholeness.

Little by little, by staying in His Word and trusting Him, God transformed my patterns, habits, and thoughts about death and life. In obedience, I pulled back a little more from life, work, and friendships so He could access me in such a way that I would be changed forever. These years have been much like the Old Testament descriptions of going into the enemy's camp and slaughtering . . . but in this case slaughtering every thought, word, action, or deed about how we define death, look at loss, and cope with grief. And as I went in, day by day as a warrior, I felt my battle wasn't just for my children or me. It was divinely inspired to plunder the enemy of lies and silence him—and profoundly—so that he loses his capacity to torment believers through grief and loss. Believers in Jesus Christ must become convinced and transformed by what is true about loss; it is then that we won't be distracted or deceived by the lies of the enemy. Our minds are renewed and we choose daily to live in *hope.* Yes, we grieve, but we grieve differently: with hope, because Jesus has purchased hope for us on the cross. We don't have to grieve as the world grieves (see 1 Thessalonians 4:13).

We are renewed creatures; again, think back to Romans 12:2. Our minds are transformed. Our sadness is the very essence of Jesus Himself, when He wept at Lazarus's tomb. He was sad, grieved, and expressed it with His tears. Remember the shortest verse in the Bible? *"Jesus wept."* He did. He modeled grief for us and it included both tears and sadness. And guess what? He expressed all of this raw emotion before He raised Lazarus from the dead! He knew what was getting ready to happen. Lazarus was—as we say in the south—fixing to be raised from the dead. Fixing to be "undead." And yet, Jesus stayed in the moment and modeled for us grieving with hope. He went to the sisters, Mary and Martha, and grieved with them and then raised their brother to life again.

You know what? He does that for every believer! He raises us up to new life! As I studied, wept, prayed through, and grieved in such a raw way for so long, God showed me that He raised David to new life that day in the hospital. David didn't come back to live on earth like Lazarus did; he actually got something better! He is walking on those streets of gold with the King of Kings and Lord of Lords! Here's the truth: David's body gave out on February 5, 2004, but his spirit went home, raising out of the dead body so he could continue eternity in another location. And someday I'll join him! Our kids, Kye, and all who are in Christ Jesus will be there! David will see our beautiful grandkids, again, because I think he got to meet them even before I did. (I like to think of it as part of the rewards or the inheritance that God gives those who trust Him.)

So verses like Proverbs 2:7, 8 don't make me cringe and question God anymore.

He holds success in store for the upright,
He is a shield to those whose walk is blameless,
For he guards the course of the just
and protects the way of his faithful ones.

God was a shield around David that rainy February morning. God did protect his faithful one because David is with Him in glory right now. You see, these promises are eternal promises, not some kind of "avoid harm" card here on earth! How silly would that be? The Proverbs 2 Scriptures are in effect the minute we give our lives to Jesus. The harmful, unsafe places aren't comparing Heaven and earth. It's a comparison of Heaven and hell! "No harm will befall us" means that when we give our lives to Jesus, then the devil, our enemy, cannot harm us any longer! He has no authority over us because we're walking in the light and being renewed daily! The finished work of the cross is *complete* in us from the moment we say yes to Jesus! And—the best news ever!—we get renewed daily, transformed, and we get continual growth, a sanctification process that continues on in us! This peace is a resounding yes! in my spirit. David relocated, transferred if you will, to another place to live. He didn't die; he kept on living. His body might have given out, but he didn't, not the *real* him. He is living today in glory! I'm sure he's been given assignments since February 5, 2004 that would amaze me! David is where all believers who place their faith in Jesus want to be. He achieved the goal! He got the prize: to be with Jesus forever.

Don't get me wrong: the death of a body is a loss. Even the death of a believer is loss. It hurts, we cry, we grieve. We are undone in our emotions until the healing comes. It's simple science: when the body sustains too much trauma or is eaten up with disease, it just gives out. It can't keep going; it dies. But for a believer in Jesus Christ, what's inside the body, our inner man, continues to live. Our spirit goes on to a final destination, dependent on the choices made by the person living in the body on earth. That's why the apostle Paul emphatically writes what the prophet Isaiah wrote earlier: "Death has been swallowed up in victory." And Paul repeated what the prophet Hosea said (Hosea 13:14): "Where, oh death, is your victory? Where, oh death, is your sting?" Paul goes on to say that the sting of death is sin, but if the blood of Jesus has redeemed our sin problem, then we have no problem and no sting in death. Jesus Christ has indeed given us the victory!

So then, is death supposed to be something that is not at all sad for believers? No! It is absolutely sad, because we miss the person who is no longer with us on earth. Remember: Jesus wept. He was touched by the sadness of the mourners and cried at the death of his friend Lazarus, who he was getting ready to raise from the dead! He cried for Mary and Martha's loss, for the other grieving relatives and friends, and for His own loss. Lazarus was His friend too, and Jesus was fully God and fully human! We are to weep at losses like this. Grief is a natural response to loss. It's OK to show the emotion you are feeling. It's how we were created, and we were created in God's image. He understands us and knows He's provided healing for our broken hearts.

TWENTY-SEVEN

Practicing What I Preach

So, as I said about the earlier part of my journey, God just keeps unpacking things and teaching me the meaning of His Word. Now when I read Proverbs 1:33, it means that I will be protected from every onslaught of the enemy and that he can never pluck me out of my Father's hand to harm me.

David wasn't harmed. David won. David got to go where I want to be. I have asked the Holy Spirit to give me revelation on what Proverbs 1:33 and others like it mean. I believe these verses are big-picture perspectives for us. Not really for this life on earth, in these bodies, but for our created life as a whole. From conception to life eternal, God preserves us from glory to glory. He sustains us and sees to it that we are never snuffed out from beginning, and through, eternity. We never have to fear when we are in Him, that we, the real us, our renewed spirit, will cease living or die. Accepting Jesus as Savior and making Him Lord gives us the complete assurance that we will have Him always and forever, down here on earth and after our time on earth has come to a close.

What are God's instructions? Jesus brought the final set when He came: that we are to love God first; and second, to love our neighbor as we love ourselves. When we love God, we accept His plan of saving us: redemption through Jesus Christ. When we take that step of faith, exchanging our life for His, eternity is guaranteed for us. We have no guilt in life and no fear in death. (These are also important lines in the hymn "In Christ Alone.") We are secure in Him, and we triumph over our foes—the enemy, Satan, and his demons of darkness. We understand that life is more than living and occupying earth. This is a holding ground for the wonderful things to come. Have you read any of the descriptions of those who've gone on to eternity and then come back from Heaven? Their words are amazing and make me excited and unafraid to relocate when God says the number of my days is through. Remember when my pastor-friend asked me this silly question:

"Why in the world would you ever think that a loving God would take a 46-year-old daddy away from his children?"

My answer that day came from a numb and completely stunned brain! "I don't know, but I guess I'll find out, because that's what I'm living." Essentially, that was my answer that day!

But what would I say to this man today? Here's a verse that speaks to my heart and refutes what that man said to me that day (John 10:27-29).

My sheep listen to my voice; I know them, and they follow me.
I give them eternal life, and they shall never perish; no one will
snatch them out of my hand. My Father, who has given them
to me, is greater than all; no one can snatch them out of my
Father's hand.

Today I would give quite a different answer.

"Oh, wounded heart. Our Father God is so big! I have found Him to be a faithful husband and most tender Father. Our children have experienced a depth with the Father God that pales in comparison to anything they'd previously experienced. We each have tasted and seen that the Lord is good. He has lavished His love on us, walked with us, provided a second husband and dad for us, and given us dreams, hopes, and visions to sustain us. We have seen miracles in our lives that only He could have orchestrated. Would we have changed any of it? I don't see how we could take any of the last twelve years and say that God didn't come through for us. Every heart-wrenching, painful, and glorious moment came through our Father's hands; He allowed them and He has defeated Satan because we are walking in victory! We have experienced the depths and heights of a loving Father. To change the events of February 5, 2004, would mean we'd have to go back, and I don't want to exchange the riches received from the Father by those in a special group: widows and orphans. And David? Well, I can't imagine that he would ever choose to come back to this earth after being in glory for the last twelve years."

So, here's the place I've landed after years of grieving, striving, learning, and loving. If you surrender to God, you don't hold anything for yourself. You give everything to Him. He's your master and commander and you've given Him complete authority. He calls the shots and He knows what's best. While I didn't expect David to have an accident and relocate to Heaven at 46, this is what my heavenly Father has allowed, and I'm surrendered to that plan. I don't ask why; I don't need to know why. I trust God. He is busy building a kingdom. He's already got the blueprint. He's building to specification, and I am fully submitted to His design and plans. Where else would I go? *He* has the words of eternal life!

TWENTY-EIGHT

When Grief Comes Back to Bite You, Again and Again

Give sorrow words. The grief that does not speak.
Whispers the o'erfraught heart and bids it break.

—Shakespeare's *Macbeth*

Don't let the title of this chapter strike fear into your heart! Remember:

Process is good.
Journeys take time.
Grief is like an onion.

Think about the structure of an onion. There are lots of layers, and they're all stinky! But leaving the layers to rot, instead of peeling them away, is unhealthy. And as painful as it is to look at grief and try to sort it out, you're much better off not to ignore it, because it's certainly not going away on its on!

Our family's waves of sadness may be fewer and fewer as time goes by, but sadness will still crash in now and again. We've each learned to look at and feel the waves of sadness and examine the truth they bear:

> *We loved David dearly.*
> *His life was precious and valuable.*
> *We each miss him, sometimes desperately,*
> *and in very different ways.*

Each sadness, every moment when the wave of sorrow washes over, must be looked at, examined, and then given over to our Savior, Jesus Christ, the only One who is bringing together the broken pieces once again, bonding them together for a usable vessel, able to hold life again.

Kye and I attend a church that values encouragement, honor, and speaking life into people. One Sunday, out of the clear blue, the pastor asked five people to come to the front of the auditorium to speak encouragement and life to them. We'd been attending this church for about two years at this point, so we didn't know a lot of people. In fact, I didn't know any of the people the pastor had called up. Then I heard a lady at the front say, "The woman in the middle section here, back several rows in the red and black swirly pattern, stand up, because God wants to bless you today!" *Whoa! Really? I could certainly use some blessing today*—this is probably similar to what I thought. So I stood up, and she began: "What's your name?" . . . "OK, Julie, I heard Isaiah 43:1, 2 over you." And the verse reads:

> *Do not fear, for I have redeemed you;*
> *I have summoned you by name; you are mine.*
> *When you pass through the waters,*

I will be with you;
and when you pass through the rivers,
they will not sweep over you (43:1, 2).

She went on.

"And I saw an umbrella, and it was a very large beach umbrella, and I believe the Lord wants you to know that you're covered. There are times when people see the rain as very scary, and there's devastation that can happen. There's also life from the watering that happens with the rain. And so, there's a blessing and a pouring down. And I think that what the Lord is doing in your life, there's nothing to be afraid of, and you're going to pass right through the waters and you are going to receive all the goodness and mercy and loveliness of the rain, and not the devastation."

I needed to hear this. I was shocked at how accurate she was. I knew that grief was stirred in my heart, but really, so many years later? It was true. I did have feelings of fear in rainstorms, and especially rainy Thursday mornings. I dreaded those days, feeling like something bad was going to happen. A foreboding, eerie feeling, an anxiousness would envelop my heart. I'd be out of sorts or really, really sad for the next few days.

How amazing that my Father doesn't want me to live in any kind of sadness, hopelessness, or fear. He has freedom for me! I'm not held captive by any of these feelings or fears. Because of His freedom, I no longer live in fear of rain or loss.

TWENTY-NINE

SOW IN TEARS, REAP IN JOY!

Getting out of the rabbit hole of grief was the best thing that ever happened to me. Daily Bible reading brought clarity, although I found it very difficult to stay focused and concentrate during that first year of grief. What I did find extremely helpful were little devotional books, where reading was short, sweet, and to the point. Bible verses that precious friends would add to a sweet card ministered to me as well. Most books I was given were put on a shelf to read later because my brain just couldn't wrap itself around them. Instead, I liked to write verses, in my own words, on index cards with different colors of Sharpie markers; I would use block print or curly Q-type letters. A verse like this one, from 2 Corinthians 5:9.

So we make it our goal to please Him,
whether we are at home in the body or away from it.

My version, how this speaks to my heart? "I make it my

goal to please God, whether I'm in my body here on earth or I'm finished with my body and in His presence."

Each day took tremendous courage and resolute determination, believing that in every moment God is bigger than my loss, my pain, or my disappointment. I said from the very beginning that my loss would not define me, but it would definitely shape me. Well that's certainly proven true in the last decade plus two years. It has shaped me; it's actually changed me for the better. I'm a much more thoughtful, understanding, compassionate, and calm person. I'm more grateful and thankful than I ever was. Instead of racing and striving my way through life, I trust God to lead me beside still waters. Life has indeed moved on, but I've moved on with it. I don't live in the past. I live in the present and have great hope for the future. I don't dwell on what I don't have; I look at all I do have. I've been blessed beyond measure with family, friends, and opportunities to serve the One who pulled me out of the pit and planted my feet on a rock.

I know I'm on the road to healing because I can actually thank God for what I've learned in the loss and pain of grief. This is an extremely important step in the road to recovery, because Proverbs 13:12 says, "Hope deferred makes the heart sick." Disappointment—or hope put off, postponed—can actually make your *heart sick*. That's insightful. Think of how many of us have been disappointed in life. We've all walked through difficulties, pain, and sorrow. To think that these disappointments can actually make us sick if we don't manage them well is quite sobering. This was actually the most dangerous path I found myself flirting with in my journey toward healing. I had to be extremely intentional in dealing with my grief and disappointment. I needed to experience it, yes, but not allow grief and widowhood to become my identity for the rest of my life! Taking on that mantle is crippling to both heart and body.

Humbling myself and learning daily how to stay at my Father's side so I could get my broken heart healed properly was the greatest challenge and blessing. My Father helped me manage my loss and led me to a place where I could honestly say, "I trust you, Father." For me, healing properly meant saying yes to the Father, Son, and Holy Spirit each and every day. It was more about making small, smart choices every day rather than looking at the big picture. I couldn't handle big-picture or long-range life goals. These moved me from faith into fear rather quickly. Questions like: What do you think your next few years look like? Well, these types of questions creeped me out. I'd think, *Gee, I don't know. I'm just trying to remember to brush my teeth!*

But when I focused on the small, positive, daily good choices, I inched down the road to peace, health, and joy much quicker than trying to figure out my life's plan. The ministering angels of Heaven assigned to me in those first six months surely applauded my daily decisions to get out of bed, make Cameron and me breakfast, and drive him to school. Daily choices like choosing forgiveness and love over bitterness and anger thrilled my heavenly Father. And when I messed up and chose poorly, He was always with me, tenderly saying, "I love you. It's all right. Get back up, and in the morning we'll try it again."

From the first day of widowhood I've given myself time to mourn. In fact, I still do! It actually took around seven years of what I call hard grieving. This is grieving that can feel anywhere on the charts: from mild sadness to paralyzing sadness, and nearly any day. My times of active mourning came in huge pendulum swings, with the eighth year having the fewest swings and the ninth year not containing any moments of total devastation. Sometimes I just feel out of sorts. Then it hits me that something has drawn me back to loss. I grieve, and I cry if I need to. I talk, look through pictures, watch the memorial video, or call David's mom or sister.

And then, it's better. I'm better. Again, this is my experience; everyone's will be different.

I still have moments when I'm afraid, but I don't have a spirit of fear that is latching itself onto me and trying to destroy me. I've come to learn that fear is a natural emotion. It tells us to run from a dangerous situation and motivates us to get to safety. But it is never meant to take hold of our lives and control us. For instance, for years after the accident I would drive down the road and have the thought that an oncoming car was going to crash into me and I would experience what David did. When they started to drive, I had the same thoughts about both Aubrey and Cameron. But I know that paralyzing, unnatural fear is not from our heavenly Father. Those thoughts are from the pit of hell and must be renounced, rejected, and sent back to the pit from which they came.

When Jesus and the disciples were in the boat, the disciples became afraid of the storm and cried out in fear. They believed they were going to drown. Jesus calmly showed them how to face the fear, calm the storms in their lives, and trust God. I practice this whenever needed: I'm quick to identify fear, call it what it is—unbelief—calm myself down, and turn to my Father. It works every time. Peace comes quickly, and all doubt, confusion, frustration, and unbelief flee.

What is your pain point? Where does the enemy feed you a lie that you take on, nourish, and accept as truth? Be on guard, because every time you listen to the lie, entertain and feed on it, it turns on you and begins to feed on *you*. That's right. We nourish these lies in such a way that they grow and flourish in our lives because we're supporting them! And after it feeds, it gets fat and happy, and then it becomes a stronghold and we begin to accept the lie as a new reality. It was never meant to become a false foundation in my life, or your life—not for one second.

I realize that some of you might be thinking: Well, this is all fine for you, Julie. You've been on this journey with God for years, so of course you are doing well after a few bumps in the road. First, those seven years of hard grieving were far from merely bumps in the road. However, it is true, I was getting myself to the Lord and becoming a fine-tuned instrument. But if you're wondering where that leaves the person who hasn't been studying God's Word for twenty-two years, I've got great news!

Read Matthew 20:1-16. If you can, stop and read it now, before continuing on.

Now, did you catch the cool part? According to Jesus' teaching, it doesn't matter how long you've been in the kingdom. We all have the same access and get the same thing! Whether you've been a Christian for two days or twenty-two years—in kingdom time, it doesn't matter! All we have to do is show up and ask Him who is able to fill our cup to complete and overflowing! What great news! Seven years into the journey, I've learned that our life on earth isn't the beginning and end.

We are all part of a much grander story than the one we see now. Our stories contain both life and death. You see, when man sinned, he was separated from God—we *all* were separated from God. The story, as we know it from the Bible, has always been about God making a way back for us. He made that way back when He sent Jesus to the cross to make the final payment, the blood-bought payment for the sins of the whole world—mine and yours. A simple way for me to look at it is on my forehead. Before I accepted Jesus, asking him to take on my sin, I had the word *death* written across my forehead. When I made that exchange, the word death was changed to *life*. I will have *life* on my forehead forever, because the blood of Jesus that never washes off, gets erased, or is taken away, marks me. This is a done deal. God will never go back on that deal no matter what I do, say, think, or feel. God has me in the palm of His hand, and He will never let go.

I may let go, but He never does, because the staying power of Christ's blood and His grip will never be broken. So when the question is life or death, that answer has been settled once and for all for those who have said yes to Jesus' purchase. That question was settled for David Hunt as a little boy in the General Baptist Church in Springfield, Missouri, where his great uncle was pastor. Nothing David said or did for the next thirty-six years of his life on earth affected his decision for salvation, his decision to come to Jesus for *life*. He was saved from his sin by accepting the blood price that Jesus gave. Period. Done. Even if David had turned his back on God, saying, "I'm done; I don't believe this anymore," it can't be undone. God cannot and will not turn away from anyone who has said with his mouth and believed in his heart, "Jesus, I'm yours. I accept the price of blood that you paid."

So, as believers in Christ, we walk solidly into eternal life *at that moment*! We do not graduate into eternal life when our bodies give out on this earth. The exchange is made when acceptance is spoken. When we say, "Jesus, I'm yours," the death sentence is erased and eternal life begins.

In *Return of the King*, the final movie in the Lord of the Rings trilogy, the wizard Gandalf's response to Pippin is a beautiful description of what we don't yet know or understand.

Pippin: I didn't think it would end this way.
Gandalf: End? No, the journey doesn't end here. Death is just another path, one that we all must take. The grey rain-curtain of this world rolls back and all turns to silver glass and then you see it . . .
Pippin: What, Gandalf? See what?
Gandalf: White shores, and beyond, a far green country under a swift sunrise.
Pippin: Well, that isn't so bad.

Gandalf: No. No, it isn't.[8]

Gandalf's description sounds familiar. It sounds a lot like Heaven. A place I'm so looking forward to relocating to. Thank you, David, for leading the way.

EPILOGUE

I sought the LORD, and he answered me;
he delivered me from all my fears.

—PSALM 34:4

The Lord heard my cry, over and over again. He gave me Himself, His peace. I find that when I choose to stay in His presence I forget about my plans and the cares of this world. I have no need to control situations because, in His presence, I experience a fullness of joy that tells me: *It does not matter.* It is a safe place; it's a good place.

I know my testimony, how God has pulled my life out of the pit and set me on a firm foundation. God has done far more than I could ask or imagine. I'm twelve years after the accident and have now been married to Kye for ten. I'm consistently living the life I dreamed I'd have way back when the wounds were fresh. Remember when I boldly cried out to God, asking Him to fill my life with greater joy?

I'm walking and living out all the prayers that those warriors, friends, family, church members, and acquaintances have lifted to Heaven. How remarkable! If you're reading this and you were among the throngs of people who lifted prayers to the Father on our family's behalf, first: Thank you! And second, your prayers have been answered!

We don't always know why bad things happen. I'm no expert on why the road we walk can be so heartbreaking. But if there's one thing I'm learning, it's this: In Christ, even in suffering, there is redemption.

Twelve years have passed since the Rainy Thursday. Aubrey has married her high school sweetheart, Brad, and they have a son, David—we all call him "Davey"—named after his Papa David. And a daughter, Julianna, named after me. Aubrey graduated from Vanderbilt with honors in biomedical engineering and two years later earned a master's degree from Peabody in secondary education. Her daddy, were he still living here, would be so thrilled with this beautiful young wife and mother, living a simple life, honoring and pleasing to God.

Cameron continued through high school and, much to all our delight, played on a championship football team! David would have been out of his mind with joy at seeing his big, strong son play award-winning football! Cameron went on to the mission field and lived out of the country for a few years. He's back and living in our area (yes, I'm thrilled!). He's had his ups and downs with grief, but I'll let him write his own book about that. He serves God faithfully, and I'm deeply moved by his depth and maturity. He also does video production like his daddy. And he's good—extremely good—at it.

The joy I have is that God's faithfulness was proven over and over to our family, and we really have increased joy out of deep sorrow! Beauty for ashes, just like God promises!

Gretta, my faithful dachshund, lived fourteen and a half years. The afternoon of her death I told her over and over what a good dog she'd been and how, even in her death, she taught me about unconditional love and devotion. I'll be honest with you, though. Her passing stirred up loss in my heart. But I met it straight up and gained victory. I love how our heavenly Father uses His creation to teach us about Himself. There must be a special place in the heart of God for our animals, and especially my feisty, female miniature dachshund!

I love God so much. My comfort is from Him, and He is sufficient. Although He doesn't take away the sorrow, He holds our hand as He leads us through it. I'm so thankful for such a tender, active place of mercy that our Father offers.

To God be all the glory! AMEN!

Appendices

HOW TO HELP FAMILIES IN GRIEF CRISIS

- When a family has experienced a loss there will usually be a central place where folks gather. Make sure this location has simple, healthy snacks and food available immediately. We found the sandwiches, ice, drinks, vegetable tray, and chips a blessing when we came home from the hospital. Other ideas include: a basket of individually wrapped granola bars, peanut butter crackers, dried fruit, and nuts. Don't forget breakfast foods like bagels, muffins, yogurt, and drinks like orange juice, coffee, tea, cream, and sweetener.

- Disposable plates, cups, and plasticware are invaluable. Add napkins, paper towels, Kleenex, and toilet paper, because there will be many people in and out of the central meeting home.

- There are several free, online meal websites that are extremely helpful in coordinating meals for the family. Both mealtrain.com and takethemameal.com are popular. A simple online search will reveal others.

- If you have a spare bedroom or two, offer a bed and breakfast for relatives and friends coming in to be with the hurting family.

- Offer to make calls, update a Facebook profile, send out an email, or, if necessary, set up a social media funding account for the family in need.

- If you're a service provider, offer your services to the family for free. A manicure/pedicure may be a special distraction for a hurting person. Offer to clean the house or change the sheets for incoming relatives.

My mother-in-law's hairstylist gave her a wash, cut, and style the week after she got home from David's service. "I don't cook or send flowers," the stylist offered. "But as you know, I can do hair." That act of love was so appreciated by Dorothy.

- There are many unique ways to express sorrow and support. Ask our Father God to show you exactly what the hurting person in your life needs in the moment. Laura, a caring heart at church, embroidered a pillowcase for me, front and back, with the words to the Nichole Nordeman song, "Every Season," which we played at David's service. This gift was a treasure to me as I buried my weary head in my pillow night after night. It was both thoughtful and lovely to give a hurting widow. And you might remember my friend Tammy, who gave me the stuffed monkey to cuddle with each day and night.

Give much thought and prayer to your gift. Don't give tickets to specific events because the hurting heart may not be up to going. Gift cards that could be used any time make better gifts. Be sensitive. People in mourning are going through the motions, whether they act normal or not. Don't give a cookbook, a pet, or yoga classes. What you think they need probably isn't what they need. That's why I say: Ask God and wait for the answer. The perfect idea may be nothing like you planned—and it may even come six months later.

WHAT NOT TO SAY TO THOSE IN GRIEF

Consider removing these phrases from your vocabulary when speaking with a person in deep grief.

"God doesn't give you more than you can handle." This little nugget is not in the Bible. Stop using it. It's not true and it sounds dismissive. Many of my days felt like more than I could handle. I needed friends who'd listen to me and not try to fix me.

"God is in control." Yes, He is. I never doubted He was. But your dismissive phrase makes me think you have no clue what to say or do in my situation.

"I know what you're going through." Really? Did you suffer a major loss today? If you haven't been through a painful situation just like the person you're trying to comfort, don't tell them you know what they're going through—because you don't.

"I'll be here for you." Unless you're going to move in and be around 24/7, don't say this. For all of us, it's unlikely we'd stick with such a promised commitment.

"Just have faith. It'll get better." Folks who say things like this are just trying to fill up the space of dead air because they're uncomfortable and want to say or do something. Believe me when I say that saying *nothing* is really better than saying any of the above things.

"Just call me if you need anything." Believe me, I had many, many needs. But I could barely get my teeth brushed every day, much less organize an army of people to help me with the practical cares of life. I likely won't call you, but you could call me and offer a service or kind word, like, "I'm thinking of you."

"They're better off in Heaven." Yes, I'm sure they are. But for now, I'd like them right here with me.

"My cousin's neighbor's little brother had cancer. It was awful!" Yes, I'm sure it was. But I have no idea why you're telling me this now. It's not helping.

"God may be saving them from a future of pain." Really? I honestly don't know if He is. And frankly, I don't think you do either.

And last: Don't ask me how I feel. Here's why: *I don't know how I feel.* Perhaps it's better to say, "I'm thinking a lot about you." Or, "I'm praying for your comfort."

WHAT TO DO FOR PEOPLE IN LOSS OR PAIN

- *Do* say: "I'm so sorry you're hurting." Believe me, that's enough. Don't feel like you must fill the silence with words.

- Sit with the hurting person and realize that silence is OK. It will probably feel awkward to you, but it probably won't to them.

- Learn to recognize the social cues they give you. If they talk, listen to them. An empathetic listener gives a wonderful gift to the hurting person. If you're asked a question, answer slowly and thoughtfully. If they are tired and need space, give it to them.

- Don't disappear. Grief is sad, but it's not contagious! The grieving person needs to be listened to and allowed to cry.

- Don't be afraid to laugh. Remember that Proverbs 17:22 says that a cheerful heart is good like medicine. Don't be insensitive, but don't be afraid of lightheartedness either.

- Everyone needs encouragement. If you admire the hurting one's strength, attitude, or sense of humor, tell them! Sincere compliments bring smiles and help alleviate stress during a difficult time. Remember, if you don't know what to say, simply tell them, "I'm thinking about you."

- Fill a specific need the person may have, like child care, groceries, a meal, or a special treat. Remember, saying "Call me if you need anything" sounds like a genuine offer, but it puts the burden of action on the hurting person and, most of the time, they won't be able to follow through. Instead, carry out specific duties.

I had a friend bring me five pastries from a very expensive bakery on Valentine's Day morning. I would have never treated myself to such extravagance, but she did it for me and I loved it.

Two months after the accident, I was ready to engage a bit more. Instead of muddling around by myself, I told two or three friends my specific needs and they took over. On a Saturday afternoon they showed up, bringing snacks, drinks, a large calendar, and their own personal calendars. They divvied up the responsibilities I needed help with, like house cleaning, grocery shopping, just sitting with me in lonely times, and helping me run my business, SmartKids 101. Those who like to cook signed up for meals; those who didn't did other things. It was beautiful and so encouraging to me!

I also asked for something we called Daily Bread. It was my idea two years earlier when a friend was going through cancer treatments and needed daily Scripture, prayer, and encouragement. A few of us rotated mornings, calling at 7:30 and giving "daily bread" to our friend. We'd spent the day before our calling asking the Father what He would like us to tell the person, and then we'd listen. Sometimes a short testimony, a devotion that meant a great deal to us, or a Scripture. And we always ended in prayer. Daily Bread was never longer that ten minutes unless the recipient wished it to be longer. The day after my family left, my friend and personal care pastor, Casey, asked if I needed anything. I told her, "Yes, will you start Daily Bread for me, like we did for James and Lois?" She was delighted to coordinate and screen those who'd be calling me. I deeply appreciated it.

- When a friend or family member relocates, we are, of course, heartbroken. And we must remember that the Father will meet the family in grief like they've never known before. God is faithful and near to the brokenhearted. Pray and look at the situation with the eyes of your heart, for you will be witnessing a testimony in the making.

The body of Christ is evident in moments like these. When one member of the body hurts, we all hurt. It's much like when our physical bodies are in pain. We're asked, "Where does it hurt"? We answer: "Well, my head hurts and I think that is making my neck and shoulders feel tight and stressed. My stomach was hurting earlier."

In the same way, our spiritual connectedness in Christ is aware when one of our brothers or sisters are hurting. We are connected in Jesus. (Romans 4:4,5 is a great verse to study.)

REMINDERS TO THE GRIEVING PERSON

- Don't be afraid to cry. Tears release emotions that we can't form into words. Cry as much or as often as you need.

- You will have moments that feel normal and OK, and then fifteen minutes later be reduced to a puddle of tears on the floor. That's normal; you're not crazy. You're grieving. Have you ever watched ocean waves? Grief comes similarly: small but steady, and sometimes crashing and fearful. Learn to flow with what your heart and mind are feeling. Express your grief. It honors your loss.

- The Trinity is at work in your life. The Father loves you, caring so deeply for your heart. Jesus is beside you and will never leave your side. The Holy Spirit is your comforter. He lives inside you and brings a new supply of comfort as often as you need. The Trinity is near to the brokenhearted. Cry, scream, question, whatever you need—God is big enough to supply it.

- It's OK to ask for help. No matter how hard or bad the day was, tomorrow is fresh and new. Hope is and will be restored to you in time, and others will consider it an honor to walk with you through this journey.

- You may think your world has ended, but it has not. Life will go on, but give yourself lots of time and be gentle with your heart. You cannot rush the process of grief. A new normal will come, but it is established ever so slowly. Also, busyness will not make the pain go away. You cannot escape the path you are on. You must travel it to move forward to healing. Take your time, but inch forward.

- Talk about the person who's gone or the situation you're facing—often. Go through the details as much as you need. Remember him or her and talk about your shared memories. Write or journal if you find that outlet helps you process. Facing your grief will help you grow through it. Running away from it or ignoring it will not help. It won't go away on its own. It will have to be dealt with at some time or it will consume you.

- Laughter is like good medicine. Don't feel guilty when you have good days, laugh, or have a general positive feeling. These days are like a balm of healing, respites of recovery for your heart and soul.

- Eat as healthy as possible. Take care of yourself. Walk, move, do things you enjoy doing when you can. Try to keep yourself open to people. Don't shut yourself off. You are still alive. And please, don't medicate your pain with alcohol, drugs, other relationships, or work. Such things will not remove your pain and could prolong your recovery. Find help when you deal with your sorrow in unhealthy ways.

- Be prepared that your grief can lend itself to irrational thoughts. Work through them with others who are trusted and close. No one will respond to your grief perfectly. I recall that I was angry when folks didn't bring up my loss, and I was angry when they did. Irrational? Maybe. Give others grace when you feel disappointment or let down by them.

- While tempted to ask "why," remember this question rarely gets answered. But asking "how" will usually spark genuine answers. How will God be glorified through my suffering? How can I express my love and appreciation for my loved ones? How can I grow through my pain?

- Remember: loss is a horrific ache and a beautiful glory. It is refining and life changing. Do not fear it. Let it teach you its deep and profound lessons.

Endnotes

1. Elisabeth Kübler-Ross, *On Death and Dying* (New York: Simon & Schuster, 1970, 2009).

2. Jars of Clay, "Something Beautiful," *The Eleventh Hour* (Essential Records, 2002).

3. J.R.R. Tolkien, author (United Kingdom: Allen & Unwin, 1954). Fran Walsh, Philippa Boyens, and Peter Jackson, screenplay, *The Lord of the Rings: The Fellowship of the Ring* (WingNut Films and The Saul Zaentz Company, 2002).

4. Nichole Nordeman, "Brave," *Brave* (Sparrow, 2005).

5. *Lars and the Real Girl* (United States and Canada: Metro-Goldwyn-Mayer, Sidney Kimmel Entertainment, Lars Productions, 2007).

6. Darlene Zschech, "All Things Are Possible," *All Things Are Possible* (Hillsong, 1997).

7. John Mark McMillan, "How He Loves," *The Song Inside the Sounds of Breaking Down* (John Mark McMillan, 2005).

8. J.R.R. Tolkien, author (United Kingdom: Allen & Unwin, 1954). Fran Walsh, Philippa Boyens, and Peter Jackson, screenplay, *The Lord of the Rings: The Return of the King* (WingNut Films and The Saul Zaentz Company, 2003).

About the Author

It was in fourth grade that Julie Hunt realized God had given her a gift of communication when her daddy affectionately nicknamed her The Newspaper.

This was, of course, due to her exceptional memory and flawless, detailed descriptions of the day's events at the nightly dinner table. While dad's nickname for her was most likely in jest, she took it as high praise, because after all, someone needed to be the family know-it-all and she was delighted to fill the position.

After high school she realized that broadcast journalism was a more efficient way to deliver the news, so Julie made plans to earn her degree in Radio-Television-Film at Oklahoma State University. She met David, her first husband, while working at a public radio station delivering the daily drive time news breaks and producing a weekly program called Oklahoma Opinions.

After ten years of marriage and juggling life as a wife with two small children, this stay-at-home mom decided to dust off her journalism skills and write a babysitting curriculum. She started with teaching the neighborhood teens a new skill set, and when the training took off David and Julie together launched Smart Kids 101.

Today, their programs—Babysitting 101, Safe Kids 101 and Polite Kids 101—through live-based teaching and online eCourses, have trained more than twenty-five thousand students in important life skills.

After David's relocation in 2004, Julie became a parenting columnist for Nashville's largest newspaper, *The Tennessean*. She continues her parenting advice in the form of blogging from her company's website, smartkids101.com.

She lives in Franklin, Tennessee with husband Kye, and they are doubly blessed to have their blended family of seven adult kids and three grandkids close by.

Julie would LOVE to speak at your next women's luncheon, conference, or book club! Her warmth, passion, and enthusiasm draw the listener in, motivating them to GET UP and live the life God has planned!

Visit her website, **thejuliehunt.com** for more information!